ALSO BY MATT MILLER

The Two Percent Solution:
Fixing America's Problems in Ways
Liberals and Conservatives Can Love

THE TYRANNY OF DEAD IDEAS

THE TYRANNY OF
DEAD IDEAS

LETTING GO OF THE OLD WAYS OF THINKING
TO UNLEASH A NEW PROSPERITY

MATT MILLER

TIMES BOOKS

HENRY HOLT AND COMPANY   NEW YORK

Times Books
Henry Holt and Company, LLC
Publishers since 1866
175 Fifth Avenue
New York, New York 10010
www.henryholt.com

Henry Holt® is a registered trademark of
Henry Holt and Company, LLC.

Library of Congress Cataloging-in-Publication Data
Miller, Matthew, 1961–
The tyranny of dead ideas : letting go of the old ways of thinking to unleash a new
prosperity / Matt Miller. — 1st ed.
    p.   cm.
Includes bibliographical references and index.
ISBN-13: 978-0-8050-8787-1
ISBN-10: 0-8050-8787-7
 1. United States—Economic conditions—2001–   2. Economics—Psychological aspects.
3. Attitude change.   4. Organizational change.   I. Title.
   HC106.83.M55   2009
   330.973—dc22   2008027801

Henry Holt books are available for special promotions and
premiums. For details contact: Director, Special Markets.

First Edition 2009

Designed by Kelly S. Too

Printed in the United States of America
1   3   5   7   9   10   8   6   4   2

For Amelia and Jody

CONTENTS

THE TYRANNY OF DEAD IDEAS

TRAPPED

Three facts are now poised to shape our economic life for a generation. First, thanks to global competition and rapid technological change, America's economy is about to face its most severe test in nearly a century. Second, our political and business leaders are doing next to nothing to prepare us to cope with what lies ahead. And third, the reason for this inaction is that our entire economic and political culture remains in thrall to a set of "Dead Ideas" about how a modern economy should work. This book is about the threat that individuals, companies, and the country face from *the things we think we know,* and about the new (and surprising) ways of thinking destined to replace these Dead Ideas so that America will continue to prosper.

The next decade will bring a collision of forces that threaten to disrupt U.S. society, sink the middle class, and call into question the political and business arrangements on which our prosperity and stability have rested for decades. These perils have little to do with the housing-related financial crisis that gripped America in the fall of 2008; in fact, the need to steer our way through this near-term credit crunch now masks longer-term economic challenges that are far more consequential. The stakes couldn't be higher: if America doesn't decisively manage these tides of change, we'll face a backlash against our economic model—which, for all its flaws, has produced more betterment for more people than any other system in human history. If this backlash proves contagious, and other advanced nations lose faith in capitalism's ability to improve the lives of ordinary people, the rich world's efforts to protect its citizens from economic change will doom the developing world to dollar-a-day poverty.

The good news is that there are ways to avert this dark scenario and to flourish. The trouble is we're not doing what we need to because of the Tyranny of Dead Ideas. By this I mean the tacit assumptions and ingrained instincts broadly shared by business executives, professionals, policy makers, media observers, and other opinion leaders regarding the way a wealthy, advanced economy like the United States should work. While current thinking about the American economy is hardly monolithic, the individuals who occupy its most influential positions subscribe to certain key premises:

- our children will earn more than we do
- free trade is "good" no matter how many people it hurts
- employers should play a central role in the provision of health coverage
- taxes hurt the economy
- "local control" of schools is essential
- people tend to end up, in economic terms, where they deserve to

These axioms have percolated through the culture for decades, becoming second nature to many of us. They determine which paths we consider, which large questions we view as settled, which possibilities we allow ourselves to imagine. And therein lies the dilemma: from the halls of government to the executive suite, from the corner store to the factory floor, Americans are in the grip of a set of ideas that are not only dubious or dead wrong—they're on a collision course with social and economic developments that are now irreversible.

As these new realities crash against what people believe, a strange intellectual chasm is revealed. It's not just ordinary people who are disoriented. The stewards of our economy themselves are lost, at least to judge from the bizarre reasoning on display in exalted precincts. Consider:

- CEOs routinely bemoan skyrocketing health care costs, saying they give foreign companies a competitive edge because governments abroad pick up these bills. Yet in the next breath most executives insist that America's government should not play a bigger role in bearing this burden. *Who else do they think is available?*

- Politicians and business leaders say we should cut taxes for most (some would say all) Americans to boost the economy. Yet America already has $40 trillion in unfunded promises shortly coming due in Social Security, Medicare, and other programs serving senior citizens—and that's before we toss in the costs of rescuing America's banking system, not to mention assorted sensible blueprints to insure the uninsured, develop clean energy, rebuild roads and bridges, extend preschool, and more. *Has anyone noticed that these numbers don't come close to adding up?*

- Everyone agrees that education is the key to improving future living standards in a fiercely competitive global economy, and that we need to lift all children, not just the most talented, to higher standards of learning and achievement. Yet in the 2008 presidential campaign, not a single major-party candidate questioned our shockingly inequitable system of school finance, which dooms schools in poor neighborhoods in ways no other advanced nation tolerates. *How are 10 million poor American children supposed to compete?*

• Top economists in both political parties perennially assure us that free trade is "good for the country," because the benefits to some Americans outweigh the losses suffered by others due to foreign competition. *But wait: Who put economists in charge of weighing the interests of one set of Americans against another?*

As puzzles and contradictions like these ricochet across boardrooms, union offices, town hall meetings, and kitchen tables, the questions ask themselves. Why are business leaders afraid or unwilling to say that we need government to play a bigger role in health care? How can top officials and their advisers call constantly for tax cuts when trillions in unpaid bills are coming due? Why do politicians pledge to "leave no child behind" while overseeing public school systems that systematically assign the worst teachers and most run-down facilities to the poor children who need great schools the most? Why do free trade's losers get only lip service even from those elected representatives who say that workers are getting the shaft?

The best explanation is not ultimately cynicism, selfishness, or indifference, nor is it really an inability to perceive and act in one's own long-term self-interest. No, the deeper ailment afflicting today's confused capitalist is intellectual inertia. In every era, people grow comfortable with settled ideas about the way the world works. It takes an extraordinary shock to expose the conventional wisdom as obsolete, and to open people's minds to a new vision of what is possible and what is necessary. Yet eventually a point is reached when what was once deemed unthinkable comes to seem inevitable. The climate of opinion is transformed by events. It happened in the Great Depression, when mass unemployment and hardship swept away long-standing taboos against government intervention in the economy. It happened during the civil rights movement, when televised horrors outraged the nation and brought a convulsion that ended legal discrimination based on race. It happened in the 1970s, when recession, oil shocks, and inflation mixed with the sense that welfare programs had spun out of control to bring a new consensus to renew capitalism's "animal spirits" via lower tax rates. But the forces of the twenty-first-century global economy, powerful as they are, haven't yet proved strong enough to topple the unquestioned ideas that continue to shape American economic life—ideas about the nature of economic progress, the role of the federal government and the corporation, and the best way to balance the risks capitalism brings with the security people seek. For now, in short, America's economic future is at risk because of the Tyranny of Dead Ideas.

I've seen the distorting influence of these ideas from the inside. As a consultant to major companies, I work with top executives across corporate America, and I have heard the doubts and anxieties they bring to such questions. I also know they're too busy running their businesses in the face of unprecedented global pressures to have "connected the dots" on all this. As a government official, I saw how ambition and fear shape political behavior and breed timid thinking unequal to our challenges. As a journalist, I've spent years moving among the voices on all sides of these debates; I've also seen how hard it is for the media to address these questions without resorting to caricatures that mask more than they explain. Together these experiences have given me multiple angles of vision with which to put the American economic mind "on the couch." The struggle to adapt to globalization is poised to dominate the next generation of business and political life. What we need now are not more out-of-touch assertions that faith in markets will see us through, nor do we need well-meaning but naive "stop-the-world" jeremiads. To get past these tired formulations and transform the way we think, we need a burst of what might be called "economic therapy," offered by an ardent capitalist to help the American economy through another of its periodic turning points.

The basic aim when our economy reaches such a crossroads is to make sure that the infamous "creative destruction" of capitalism doesn't destroy so much for so many that America's embrace of innovation and economic change is also a casualty. This isn't a new worry, of course. The quest for a better blend of growth and justice has preoccupied reformers since the dawn of the industrial age. But reform is never easy. "Devotees of capitalism are often unduly conservative," wrote John Maynard Keynes in 1926, "and reject reforms in its technique, which might really strengthen and preserve it, for fear that they may prove to be first steps away from capitalism itself." Today, after America's own recent experiments, there is much we already know. We know that old-style "big government" liberalism in America is dead, and that its traditional social democratic cousin in Europe seems a poor model, having produced record rates of joblessness even as it breaks the bank. We also know that Bill Clinton's vaunted "Third Way" came and went without reducing the insecurity that Americans feel in a global age. Yet it is equally clear that the latest conservative "strategy"—cutting taxes (mostly for the well off), standing idle while health costs soar and the ranks of the uninsured swell toward 50 million, mortgaging our future to nations like China via massive trade deficits, and deregulating our financial system with explosive results—has torpedoed our public finances and fueled a pervasive sense of foreboding.

In this anxious environment, when the traditional alternatives seem exhausted, we need a new way of thinking. And, as history and luck would have it, we are on the cusp of the next of those epochal shocks that opens our minds wide enough to discover it.

PRESENT SHOCK

The shock will be administered by four forces that are set to accelerate in the next decade. The first of these—call it *White Collar Anxiety*—refers to the fact that jobs higher up the income scale (engineers, financiers, consultants, doctors, lawyers) will for the first time be exposed to competition from places like China and India. Alan Blinder, a professor of economics at Princeton University and a former member of the Council of Economic Advisers under President Clinton, estimates that as many as 40 million American jobs may be vulnerable in the coming decades, including many assumed to be immune to such threats. It's been hard enough to maintain a consensus for free trade and technological change as lower-paid manufacturing and service jobs have moved overseas. How will business and politics be reshaped when hungry foreign rivals set wage levels (and trigger "downward mobility") for better-educated and politically potent groups in ways not previously imaginable?

The second force—*The Rush for the Exits*—is corporate America's desire to stop providing health care and pensions to its employees. To be sure, these costs are soaring in ways that seem unsustainable, especially when competing firms in other nations bear fewer of them. Still, American business leaders act today as if their search for an "exit strategy" on benefits is the end of the conversation. What happens to the millions of workers who are left unprotected if companies simply walk away?

The third force is *The Gray Boomer Fiscal Squeeze*—meaning the way the aging members of the baby boom generation will shortly send government's health and pension costs through the roof. The result, at current levels of taxation, is that even "big" government will be strapped, with little cash to devote to the other public purposes we expect it to support, from border security to schools to basic scientific research. Nor will the federal government be in a position to broaden its safety net as corporate America withdraws its own. Will it simply abandon these vital functions? If not, how will it cope without raising taxes to levels that wreck economic growth?

The fourth force is the rise of *Extreme Inequality*. Even as the three forces listed above raise risks for most Americans, the very top of the wealth and income scale is pulling away at levels never before seen. Yet it's clear that many of the winners are reaping the rewards not of the "free market," but of clubby, manipulated schemes that are as likely to reward failure as success. Bankers who pocketed millions peddling subprime mortgages retire to their country clubs while the rest of us are left holding the bag. CEOs who preside over tumbling stock prices routinely walk away with tens of millions for their trouble; hedge fund managers who barely beat the S&P commonly earn such princely sums in a year. At what point does the ubiquity of the undeserving rich become so corrosive in a democracy that it sparks a backlash that wrongly discredits capitalism altogether?

The collision of these forces will expose much of our traditional thinking as dangerously flawed. It will also hurtle us toward a moment when fundamental questions are up for grabs in ways not seen since the aftermath of World War II, when the architects of a new economic order sat down to chart a course beyond depression and war. Can middle-class societies be sustained in wealthy nations in an era of globalization? Can democracy survive the emergence of extreme inequality? How will these trends affect our posture toward the hopes of the developing world? Can Americans build secure and happy lives amid this tumult?

SIX DEAD IDEAS

The answers to these questions will depend on how quickly we escape the pernicious influence of six Dead Ideas:

- **The Kids Will Earn More Than We Do.** Broadly rising incomes have been considered an American birthright. This pattern of generational advance is now at risk for as much as half the population.

- **Free Trade Is "Good" (No Matter How Many People Get Hurt).**
  Though millions of people may be hurt by foreign competition,
  we're told, the overall gains from free trade so outweigh any downside that it is folly to question its ultimate advantages.
- **Your Company Should Take Care of You.** Business (not government) must fund and manage much of our health and pension benefits, this idea holds, or else we risk becoming socialist.
- **Taxes Hurt the Economy (and They're Always Too High).**
  The truth is that taxes are going up no matter who is in power in
  the next decade, and the economy will be fine. We won't turn
  into France or Sweden.
- **Schools Are a Local Matter.** Americans need more skills to
  maintain our living standards as developing economies rise up to
  compete with us. America also spends more on schools than
  nearly every other wealthy nation—with worse results. Yet our
  unique model of "local control" and funding of schools remains
  sacrosanct.
- **Money Follows Merit.** The most cherished illusion of today's
  educated class is that market capitalism is a meritocracy—that is,
  a system in which people basically end up, in economic terms,
  where they deserve to.

As we'll see, the persistence of these Dead Ideas generally
involves a *failure to adapt to new circumstances,* a recurring feature of
human thought and behavior. In that sense, these outworn con-
cepts are part of a broader phenomenon that afflicts every organization and each of us as individuals. The question at the heart of
this book—"Are old ways of thinking preventing America from
adapting to the challenges now posed by globalization?"—is thus
surprisingly kin to such questions as "Why didn't newspapers realize more quickly that the Internet posed a fundamental threat to
their business?" and even to questions like "Why doesn't John see

that Emily's new job means that he needs to help more with the kids?" In each instance, intellectual and emotional inertia traps people in antiquated ways of thinking even though circumstances radically change. You can't develop a strategy for a country or a company (let alone for yourself) if you're blinded by preconceptions that no longer reflect the real world.

When the day of reckoning comes for a Dead Idea, things can change very quickly—and also very painfully. In the fall of 2008, for example, we witnessed the dramatic implosion of the idea that "Financial Markets Can Regulate Themselves." Within a matter of weeks, as markets tumbled and seemingly impregnable financial institutions collapsed, old ideas and convictions had to be tossed aside and massive new government interventions put in place by an ideologically conservative administration that only days before had deified free markets. If this Dead Idea had been uncovered and exploded earlier, a great deal of turmoil and suffering could have been avoided. In much the same way, other Dead Ideas are waiting now to ensnare us if we fail to open our minds and to act. What's more, while the fallout from today's financial crisis is serious, it will also be temporary; the system will almost certainly be restored to health within a few years. In the longer term, the consequences of failing to bury the Dead Ideas at the core of this book are far greater.

Our aim in the pages ahead, therefore, is to unearth premises so deeply ingrained in American economic life that they've essentially become invisible. They're just "the way things are." We're going to dig these ideas up, brush off the dirt, turn them over in the light, and assess why they no longer make sense. Moreover, it's perfectly safe to try this at home. Breaking free of Dead Ideas entails three steps:

FIRST: IDENTIFY THE DEAD IDEAS THAT MATTER.   At any given time there are dozens of Dead Ideas in our public life, and hundreds if not thousands across our business and personal lives. Truth is, most of us probably couldn't get through the day without a few Dead Ideas.

In my professional life, for example, I cling to the idea that "Rational Analysis Can Lead to Constructive Change"—which, if you've read any history, may never have been that "alive" an idea in the first place. But only a handful of Dead Ideas are big enough to pose fundamental threats; fewer still have the power to shape the fate of a society. Until the middle of the nineteenth century, for example, millions of Americans believed that "An Economy Based on White Human Beings Owning Black Human Beings Is Moral and Sustainable." This idea seems grotesque and preposterous to us now, but it determined the contours of countless lives. Similarly, before 1920 it was perfectly reasonable in the United States to think that "Democracy Does Not Require Extending the Vote to Women." Before 1913, when the Federal Reserve was established, sophisticated businesspeople believed that "Economic Stability Can Be Maintained Without a Central Monetary Authority." Today, on the international scene, many Western societies believe that "The United Nations Security Council Should Have the Same Permanent Members It Had in 1945," even though Britain and France are arguably less consequential in global affairs than rising powers like India. The list goes on.

Since there are so many potential Dead Ideas to choose from, the key in any effort to improve the prospects of a country or a company is to focus on the ones that are truly *strategic*. We need to step back from the rush of events to identify the premises that are central to an entity's fate. For a company it may be assumptions about key customers or competitors or technologies. ("Japan Will Never Be Able to Compete with American Car Manufacturers" was an idea that needed puncturing in 1980, for example.) For an individual it may involve a tough-minded assessment of personal strengths and weaknesses. For the United States as it strives to adapt successfully to the twenty-first-century global economy, the six Dead Ideas in this book have the combination of high stakes and "sacred cow" status that give them the power to derail America's future success.

SECOND: UNDERSTAND EACH DEAD IDEA'S "STORY." We can't move past a Dead Idea without first understanding the source of its power. Where did it come from? Why did it once seem to make sense? What has changed that now makes it useless or wrong or harmful? Who has a stake in its persistence nonetheless? We'll examine these and related questions through a mini-biography of each Dead Idea in part one of the book. The mere act of reviewing the history and trajectory of an idea, and dissecting the assumptions and circumstances that gave rise to it, almost immediately opens our minds to alternative ways of thinking that make more sense.

THIRD: REACH FOR NEW (AND PARADOXICAL) WAYS OF THINKING. The final step, based on a clear-eyed assessment of current trends, is to identify the new ways of thinking that are not only needed to thrive but almost certain to come to pass because they better reflect new realities. As we'll see in part two of the book, these "Destined Ideas" often seem taboo or paradoxical, because conventional wisdom has become so disconnected from the facts that ideas that should be obvious (or soon will be) appear counterintuitive or startling or otherwise "off." Don't be fooled: the fact that they appear this way only speaks to how skewed our vision has become. It's helpful to frame these Destined Ideas as paradoxes, because doing so forces us to reconcile apparent contradictions that exist only because our thinking today is faulty. As we'll see when we get to such Destined Ideas as "Only Government Can Save Business," "Only Business Can Save Liberalism," and "Only Higher Taxes Can Save the Economy," the mental exercise of embracing paradoxes has the power to stretch our minds as well.

Identify the Dead Ideas that matter; understand each one's story; and reach for new and paradoxical ways of thinking. This process is so straightforward, it's difficult to understand why we keep getting trapped in Dead Ideas. But we shouldn't be too hard on ourselves. The perils of orthodoxy at moments of sudden or pervasive change have been with us forever. The blind spots bred by complacency or arrogance or certitude or habit fill the obituaries of civilizations that didn't make it, businesses that didn't make it, even marriages that didn't make it. It's human nature. And it's the things we think we know (but don't) that are the chief obstacles to success in nearly every endeavor. In the end, however, the true measure of a person, an organization, or a society isn't the Dead Ideas we fall prey to. It's whether we can summon the perspective and imagination to recognize the Dead Ideas in our midst, and bury them before real damage—or more damage—is done.

PART ONE

TODAY'S
DEAD IDEAS

1

THE KIDS WILL EARN
MORE THAN WE DO

In which we learn that downward mobility for millions
is a new fact of American life, forcing us to think in
new ways about "progress" in order to thrive

The voters in the town hall meeting were so quiet you could almost hear them straining to listen. No public official, let alone a newly sworn-in president, had ever talked to them this way.

"Look," said the president, walking across the stage with a microphone in hand, "here's what no one wants to tell you. Structural changes in our economy, and new competition as countries like China and India rise abroad, mean that we're in a different world now. That pattern we once took for granted, in which our incomes basically kept rising across the board, turns out to be something we can't sustain. Many of you are earning less than your parents did, and the truth is, many of your children will earn less than you do." The president paused, watching as the words sank in. "Now, we can pretend this isn't the case. Most people in Washington think we're better off doing exactly that. But I don't think denial helps any of us. I know it won't help us come together to do the things we need to do as a nation to thrive even amid these new realities."

Don't worry, you didn't miss the news; the scene above never happened. No politician would say these things even if he believed them to be true, because they challenge a notion at the heart of the American dream: the idea that the kids will earn more than we do. This idea has been at the core of American experience for so long that it seems to us the natural order of things, a brand of progress to which we're practically entitled. Wave after wave of immigrants, after all, found the streets in America were paved with gold, at least over the long run. Their children found they could rise further in a vibrant economy. Little wonder that in time this expectation became embedded in the American mind. Assuring that our children rose above us became a defining feature of a family's success, and our chief measure of a satisfactory economy. Political leaders, who hold up a reliable mirror to the convictions of their followers, plainly believe we cherish this prospect, because it is central to how they talk about our lives. If someone even suggests that economic progress is eroding, they resist the possibility with a passion that suggests how deeply they feel we all *need* to believe in this idea. It's as if relinquishing the certitude that the kids will earn more than we do would be to give up something essential in the American spirit. "We won't be the first generation in American history to leave our children worse off," runs the familiar cry. We can redeem the promise of the American dream, we're told. We can hold on.

The problem, however, as new research shows, is that we've already crossed the Rubicon. As many as 100 million Americans now live in families that are earning less in real terms than their parents did at the same age. The rise of such developing economies as China and India means this earnings picture is only likely to get worse. One in three American jobs may be exposed before long to competition from workers overseas, putting an effective wage cap on large swaths of employment even if jobs don't actually move offshore. New research also shows that, contrary to popular myth, upward mobility—the ability to rise from the station into which you are born—is now lower in the United States than in many European countries. To be sure, for the immigrants who make up 12 percent of the population, it remains the case that America is the land of opportunity, where people who arrive with little but pluck and drive can rise. But the other 88 percent confront a striking new reality: ingrained assumptions about generational progress in America no longer hold, and before long may be at risk for nearly half the population.

"An important foundation of American life is mass upward mobility, in which each generation does better than the last, and people see gains in purchasing power throughout their career, and gains over what their parents earned at a similar age," says Frank Levy, an economist at the Massachusetts Institute of Technology who studies these trends. "If we've evolved to a situation where most productivity gains are going to the very top of the income distribution, and most people don't experience that mass upward mobility, then we're undermining an important feature of American life." (It's important to note that as long as the overall economy grows, so will income per person, meaning that Americans *on average* will earn more than the previous generation did. But the highest earners, who are reaping nearly all of the gains from growth in today's economy, will skew that average, meaning that for many middle-class and working-class Americans, the next generation will be earning less.)

People sense what's unfolding, even if it remains politically taboo to say it. A July 2007 survey by the Pew Global Attitudes Project found that 60 percent of Americans expect the next generation will be worse off than theirs, versus 31 percent who expect they will be better off. The persistence in our public life of a national self-image at odds with these private anxieties inhibits virtually any serious discussion of what we might do about the situation.

Yet the truth is that these developments, while hardly what we would choose, are not something to fear, and will not prove as ominous as many of us seem to imagine. Yes, they represent a jolt to our expectations and an unsettling break with our history. But if we approach the future with fresh eyes, the tests we now face will present an opportunity to fix serious flaws in our economy that have long been ignored because of our faith in the ever-rising tide. Seen in this light, our biggest problem isn't the economic change that is upon us, but the way that our outdated thinking prevents us from responding forcefully in this new situation to improve people's lives.

No one takes pleasure in the prospect that many Americans will face harder times as the country adjusts to the rise of new economic powers and sweeping new technologies. But to move forward we must first face facts. Liberating ourselves from the Dead Idea that the kids are sure to earn more than we do will force us to reexamine a fundamental question that almost never gets explicitly discussed: What is the role of the individual, and what should be the role of the broader community, in assuring opportunity and security in a wealthy nation like the United States? As events force us to consider fresh answers to this question, the result will be a good life, and in some ways a better life, even for Americans who face wage strains. When the dust clears, moreover, America will not have lost its native optimism. It will have gained the sturdier brand of hope that comes from dealing squarely with unpleasant realities rather than wishing them away.

THE BIG BANG

Why do Americans think a better standard of living for their children is a national birthright? Because this remarkable pattern has largely been our experience since the nation's earliest days. From the start, this striking record represented a sharp break with previous economic history, and with the humbler expectations people once held. A quick (and selective) trot through a few key episodes of America's economic journey helps make clear why the assumption that the kids will earn more than we do has deep roots in the American mind.

In the beginning, or at least going pretty far back, the idea of economic progress was meaningless, because there was none. "From the earliest times of which we have record," wrote John Maynard Keynes in 1930, "back, say, to two thousand years before Christ, down to the beginning of the eighteenth century, there was no very great change in the standard of life of the average man living in the civilized centers of the earth." Some periods were a little better, some a bit worse, but overall there were no important movements in average incomes over some forty centuries. Keynes ascribed this general stasis to "the remarkable absence of technical improvements" and "the failure of capital to accumulate" for growth-fueling investment. It's a stunning thought. Older Americans today can recall youths spent without commercial air travel, indoor plumbing, television, polio vaccines, long distance phone service, and countless other life-improving inventions. The idea that 150 generations once passed without a meaningful rise in living standards seems hard to fathom. But thus it was.

Then, in the late eighteenth and early nineteenth century, two powerful sets of forces converged to create a uniquely American creed of economic progress and generational betterment. Think of it as a sociological "Big Bang," with two critical ingredients: the founding of the United States itself, and the advent of the Industrial Revolution.

Take America first. The new republic's official policy of classlessness and ethic of equal opportunity made it unique in history. To be sure, from our vantage point today, many groups were excluded from this vision, including, most shamefully, African-Americans. But it's hard to overstate the breakthrough represented by America's foundational commitment to the idea that "all men are created equal," with an inalienable right to "life, liberty and the pursuit of happiness." Alexis de Tocqueville, though cognizant of variations in wealth and status in the young republic, found it telling in the 1830s that America didn't require its lowly born to acknowledge their inferiority or to bow to superiors. Tocqueville also caught the economic mood when he wrote that ordinary Americans seemed to shine with "the charm of anticipated success."

In short, America was about upward mobility, the chance to rise from the station into which you were born to whatever heights your talents and efforts might let you attain. This helps explain why America came to lead the world in mass education not long after its founding. American mores also reflected this zest for improvement. Hard work and economic ambition were seen as proper pursuits for a moral person, not frowned upon as vulgar or wicked, the opinion of European aristocrats and clergy. This judgment was echoed in the sociologist Max Weber's seminal account of how "the Protestant ethic" helped fuel the rise of American capitalism. The spirit was exemplified by Benjamin Franklin, the self-made publisher, politician, scientist, and diplomat, whose homey sermons on work, frugality, and thrift in *Poor Richard's Almanac* were wildly popular. But the most sublime and enduring emblem of America's ethos of advancement was our sixteenth president, Abraham Lincoln.

IT'S THE ECONOMY, ABE

Lincoln forever seared the idea of economic progress into our national psyche. That a self-taught rail-splitter born in a log cabin could rise to the White House proved something marvelous about America, as Lincoln himself knew. "Nowhere in the world is presented a government of so much liberty and equality," he told soldiers on their way home to Ohio in 1864. "To the humblest and poorest among us are held out the highest privileges and positions.

The present moment finds me at the White House, yet there is as good a chance for your children as there was for my father's."

"Twenty-five years ago I was a hired laborer," Lincoln told a group on another occasion. "The hired laborer of yesterday labors on his own account today, and will hire others to labor for him tomorrow. Advancement—improvement in condition—is the order of things in a society of equals."

This passion for individual advancement shaped Lincoln's approach to the slavery question in ways that we tend to forget. As he maneuvered in pursuit of the presidency in the late 1850s, Lincoln focused not so much on the morality of slavery (though he believed it wrong), but on the fate of Northern white laborers if slavery was extended to new states. After all, Lincoln argued repeatedly, how could men settling in these places ever improve their lives (and wages) if they had to compete with slaves who earned nothing? For the sake of the white working man's prospects, he concluded, the line on slavery's extension had to be drawn. This shrewd framing of the issue, which aligned the average man's economic interests with the moral fervor of abolitionists whose goals far outran public opinion, helped catapult Lincoln to the White House.

The historian Richard Hofstadter reminds us that by articulating the stakes this way, Lincoln made the Civil War not about slavery per se but about defending popular government as "a system of social life that gives the common man a chance." Lincoln

spoke for those millions of Americans who had begun their lives as hired workers—as farm hands, clerks, teachers, mechanics, flatboat men, and rail splitters—and had passed into the ranks of landed farmers, prosperous grocers, lawyers, mechanics, physicians, and politicians. Theirs were the traditional ideals of the Protestant ethic: hard work, frugality, temperance, and a pinch of ability applied long and hard enough would lift a man into the propertied or professional class and give him independence and respect if not wealth and prestige.

For Lincoln, Hofstadter concludes, "the vital test of a democracy was economic—its ability to provide opportunities for social ascent to those born in its lower ranks."

The historian Jim Cullen adds that for Lincoln, "the true end was the American dream"—not abolition, and not the union of the states. Lincoln saw the Civil War preserving "a place where upward mobility would thrive without hypocrisy or the challenge of alternative ideologies that would subvert it." If Ben Franklin was an Old Testament prophet of the dream of upward mobility, Cullen concludes, "Lincoln was its Jesus Christ."

ONWARD AND UPWARD

Yet when it came to the advancement of society as a whole, all the individual opportunity in the world might have meant little had America's early years not also coincided with the kickoff of the Industrial Revolution. This made the idea of economic progress something that applied on a grand scale to entire nations, not just to particular people with moxie and drive. Thanks to a mysterious alchemy of cultural readiness, engineering creativity, and legal protections (such as patents), advances that altered entire industries began to appear in an extraordinary burst around this time. Inventions from the spinning wheel to the steam engine spurred startling leaps of productivity in textiles, mining, chemicals, machine tools, coal, iron, and more.

The unfolding industrial ascent was matched by a new way of thinking about history's trajectory. Until this time, history had generally been regarded as cyclical, a series of situations that repeated themselves endlessly. The Bible spoke of periods of war and periods of peace, and of good harvests and bad harvests, with no notion of "progress." Empires and civilizations rose and fell: think Persia, and Greece, and Rome. The rise of science, and science's capacity to bear fruit for industry, changed this outlook. The idea of economic progress came straight out of the Enlightenment, when "useful knowledge"—what we call science and technology today—showed itself to be the wellspring of sustainable advances in human society.

Keynes's endless night of stagnation was over. Beginning around 1820, the amount of income the U.S. economy produced per person—per capita GDP—began to take off. It has grown ever since at an average of more than 50 percent every twenty-five years.

The experience of "more" led ordinary Americans to *expect* more. Karl Marx wasn't happy about this. An avid America-watcher, Marx noted that economic growth and the open frontier produced high rates of social mobility, something that Europe, with its feudal past and more rigid classes, didn't enjoy. He worried that this might stave off the socialist revolution he sought. "Though classes, indeed, already exist," Marx wrote anxiously of the United States in the 1850s, "they have not yet become fixed, but continually change and interchange their elements in a constant state of flux." His colleague Friedrich Engels observed in the 1880s that America seemed to be a nation "without a permanent and hereditary proletariat."

But if the workingman's plate was full enough to keep socialism at bay, and immigrants found opportunities to build a better life for their families, there were setbacks and pockets of suffering. Horace Greeley's famous injunction "Go west, young man" was originally a bit of career advice after the Panic of 1837, a financial meltdown that battered the nation. Between the Civil War and World War I, there were at least five significant panics or depressions—in 1873, 1884, 1890, 1893, and 1907. The depression that began in 1893 was particularly severe. Fully 18 percent of the working-age population was jobless; by 1895, the incomes of a large proportion of the population had fallen to the levels first reached in 1880.

These reversals of fortune offer important lessons for today's debates, because they led affected groups to rebel against the mainstream faith in economic advance and offer alternative visions of progress that resonate even now. Farmers, who faced long, painful periods of price declines in the second half of the nineteenth century, led the way. Along with independent craftsmen and artisans, farmers saw their economic position being eroded by forces beyond their control—big business, industrialization, urbanization. The American creed of self-sufficiency no longer seemed to pay; the virtues that bred upward mobility, long preached by Thomas Jefferson, Andrew Jackson, and Abraham Lincoln, couldn't save many of these people from being crushed. So they took action themselves. It is significant that the Populist movement, perhaps the most important democratic movement of the era, took form in *opposition* to innovation and "progress." While the Populists' "stop the world" posture did not prevail, many of the reforms they sought in order to preserve the little guy's voice and buffer the impact of industrialization—the graduated income tax, the eight-hour day, regulation of business, the initiative and referendum, direct election of senators— were enacted by the Progressives in the ensuing decades. As global economic integration continues, and it becomes clear in the years ahead that more and more people who "work hard and play by the rules" are not getting ahead in traditional American terms, the spirit of this Populist critique, alongside updated versions of its reform agenda, seems certain to be resurrected.

BOOM!

The twin tragedies of the Depression and World War II interrupted the general march of progress, but the remarkable boom that followed made earlier norms of generational economic advance seem timid. From 1945 until the early 1970s, the U.S. economy grew at an unprecedented rate. Productivity, defined as output per hour of work, which determines earnings and living standards, surged. Real incomes doubled in a generation. Americans at all income levels shared in the gains. Poverty rates fell dramatically. College attendance and graduation rates soared. The period has understandably become enshrined in discussions of the American economy as a "golden age."

Yet in retrospect, despite the achievements of the boom, the entire episode was in a real sense a historical accident, the result of the United States being the only economy left standing after a devastating global war. Consider: by 1950, though most of the reconstruction of Europe and Japan had been completed, the United States still accounted for 60 percent of the output of the seven biggest capitalist countries. Foreign competition was virtually nonexistent. Families who'd been through two wars and a depression in thirty years were bursting to enjoy life, and greeted American manufacturers with long-suppressed appetites for cars, refrigerators, washing machines, televisions, air conditioners, lawn mowers, air travel, and more. New highways spawned new suburbs and a building boom. Meanwhile, the federal government, pushing full employment and subsidizing the health and pension benefits increasingly offered by U.S. firms, made it a great time—perhaps the best time ever—to be an American worker. "Keeping up with the Joneses" became something of a middle-class obsession, as the boom unleashed a competitive consumption spree. Cheerleading for the good times pervaded the culture. Ronald Reagan, a pitchman for General Electric on television, would hold up a vacuum cleaner, flash his magical smile, and proclaim, "Progress is our most important product."

Yet this wasn't just the magic of the market. A number of other institutions helped assure that prosperity was broadly shared.

Labor unions, a robust minimum wage, progressive taxes, and a sense of restraint on corporate boards regarding the salaries of chief executives all contributed to a sense of a shared economic destiny. So too did active presidential intervention, as when John F. Kennedy angrily insisted that steelmakers rescind profiteering price increases after he had successfully urged the steel unions to restrain wage demands in 1962. In addition, improvements in central banking—whose earlier mistakes had caused and prolonged the Great Depression—made economic expansions much longer and recessions briefer and less painful than in earlier eras.

As the postwar prosperity unfolded, all this gave ordinary people a greater sense of security. The rising tide kept rising. People began to expect it would continue. In such a nirvana, a central tenet, which went without saying, was that the kids—everyone's kids— would keep earning more than their parents did. For Americans, that was simply the way life worked.

WHAT PROSPERITY WROUGHT

How did America's long record of broadly shared economic growth and upward mobility shape our national psychology and attitudes? The impact has been profound, and largely positive. Since early in the nineteenth century, foreign observers have remarked on the extraordinary optimism and entrepreneurial energy Americans possess. Our "can-do" spirit and "anything is possible" determination tamed the frontier, helped win two world wars, invented countless technologies that benefited the world, and put a man on the moon. But the way our success mutated over time into the expectation that our kids would continue to do even better has created three problematic ways of thinking that now hold America back.

The first is that we've overestimated the power of the individual to shape his own economic destiny. The thread running through our admiration of Benjamin Franklin and Abraham Lincoln on to such modern icons as Bill Gates, Ronald Reagan, Bill Clinton, and Barack Obama is the celebration of the self-made man. This toasting of such ascents from humble or inauspicious beginnings has been joined by the conviction that our heroes are merely outsized versions of the possibilities within every American's reach. In Horatio Alger's rags-to-respectability protagonists, as well as more ambiguous literary strivers like Jay Gatsby, lies the sentiment that beats also in every immigrant heart: in America you shape your own destiny via determination and hard work. America is and always has been the land of "rugged individualists." The corollary of our faith in the individual has been a tendency to judge harshly those who fail: after all, with so much opportunity for the taking, if you can't make it in the United States, it's probably your own fault. Over the course of the nineteenth century, the historian Scott Sandage observes, "Financial failure went from being an event that happens in your life to being something that defines your identity. A 'loser' in 1820 was literally a person who lost money in a business—the person who got the short end of the stick, the loser by the deal. But by the end of the nineteenth century, a 'loser' is a person who is completely worthless in every way." One can draw a line from this evolving perception to the popular antipathy toward the "undeserving poor" in the debates over welfare reform in the 1980s and 1990s.

America's emphasis on self-reliance and individual responsibility has had obvious benefits. But our equation of economic weakness or vulnerability with worthlessness helped retard the development of social protections that spread across Europe more than a hundred years ago. The need for a collective response in the face of larger economic forces has always been minimized and scorned in the individualist United States. The question is whether our instincts here have been shaped by a faith in individual economic ascent that no longer accurately describes the prospects of even many hardworking Americans in the global economy.

The second problematic way of thinking, bred especially by our extraordinary postwar prosperity, is what the author and columnist Robert Samuelson has called America's sense of "entitlement." In this view, we became so spoiled by progress that we presumed endless growth was simply our due—and believed further that this growth would enable us to solve virtually every social problem, from poverty to racial animus to health inequities. This is the economic face of American exceptionalism, the idea that the United States is somehow destined to be blessedly immune from the travails that ordinary nations face. It's the hubris that economists and business leaders began to exude during the postwar boom, when they (wrongly) opined that the business cycle could be tamed and recessions eliminated entirely. It's the culture of ever-expanding rights with little thought to associated responsibilities. Over the decades, this heady sensibility, born of affluence, spawned a cycle of inflated expectations ("wars" on poverty, crime, drugs, cancer) followed by inevitable disappointments, contributing to a loss of faith in institutions and leaders who couldn't make good on the unreasonable demand to vanquish every social ill. The distrust of government that has become the legacy of such hubris makes the work of reform harder today, because a high burden of proof is imposed on those who would use government for new purposes.

There's a third worrisome attitude traceable to our faith that the kids will earn more than we do. This is the imprudent conviction that we can live beyond our means because somehow we'll earn enough later to deal with any problems. This outlook represents a dramatic shift from earlier American thinking, as the sociologist Daniel Bell noted in 1976. "Twentieth century capitalism wrought a . . . startling sociological transformation," he wrote, "the shift from production to consumption as the fulcrum of capitalism." Bell went on:

> This was the rise of consumer durables: automobiles, refrigerators, television sets, washing machines and dryers, and the like. And all this created the revolution in retailing, particularly . . . the invention of the installment plan, the most "subversive" instrument that undercut the Protestant ethic. Against the fear of going into debt, there was now the fear of not being credit worthy. Instead of saving for the good things of life, one could buy them now and pay later. Marketing and hedonism . . . became the motor forces of capitalism.

Both as individuals and as a society, we've been running the economy a bit like a giant Ponzi scheme, gambling on better days tomorrow to make good on unsustainable borrowing today. The litany is familiar. The government has run up a $9 trillion national debt, has made $40 trillion in unfunded health care and pension promises to senior citizens, and has tolerated unprecedented trade deficits that must at some point be reversed in a consumption-cutting day of reckoning. Meanwhile, families rack up record levels of debt—mortgages, home equity loans, payday lending, credit card balances—while saving next to nothing for retirement. Business has joined the bandwagon, with corporate debt rising in recent years, and bankruptcy, once a mark of shame, now often viewed as a shrewd strategy for solving financial problems.

Such is the contemporary toll of a Dead Idea. We've overestimated the individual's control; we've felt entitled to "more" and become disillusioned at its absence; and we've grown addicted to debt-fueled consumption. These habits of mind, the fruit of our faith in a dying American dream, leave us ill equipped to cope with the economic realities we now face.

THE NEW NORMAL

The erosion of America's outsized dominance in the world economy, along with changes we still don't fully understand in the way technology shapes the nature of work, has led to unsettling developments. Economic inequality has been rising to levels not seen since the 1920s, with the top 1 percent reaping nearly all of the gains from continued productivity growth across the economy. Wages for male workers have stagnated for three decades; household incomes have risen modestly only because of the flood of women into the workforce. While these trends have been debated for several years, optimists have fallen back on a familiar trope, arguing that wage stagnation isn't cause for worry because of America's proud legacy of upward mobility; on this reasoning, even if thirty-year-old men are earning less than their counterparts did in the 1970s, it's not a problem, because over their lives men rise from lower to higher places on the income ladder. Today's wage levels, these analysts also argue, are skewed downward by the recent influx of lower-earning immigrants. Until recently these benign interpretations seemed plausible. But the latest research suggests that this hopeful view of the data was unjustified.

What's new are studies that compare nonimmigrant parents and children in the same family over two generations, analyses made possible because of something called the Panel Study of Income Dynamics, run by the Institute of Social Research at the University of Michigan. Since 1968 this survey has followed some eight thousand families from their youth into adulthood; for the first time it enables direct matching of family income of parents in the late 1960s with their children's family income in recent years. In 2008, the Brookings Institution, as part of the nonpartisan Economic Mobility Project of the Pew Charitable Trusts, mined this data to reveal that one in three Americans, of all races and at all income levels, now live in families that earn less than their parents did. This finding is more disturbing when you consider that families work longer hours today thanks to the rise of two-earner families. That's anywhere from 75 million to 100 million Americans living in families earning less than their parents did. One in three people whose parents earned the equivalent of $55,000 to $72,000 in 1968 now earn less than their parents did; one in two whose parents earned the equivalent of $100,000 back then have faced earnings losses relative to their parents as well. It's old news that individual workers face "downward mobility" when, say, good manufacturing jobs move overseas. The new downward mobility—between generations, within families—is something much broader, and far more threatening to an idea that has been at the core of America experience and thinking. "What it means," says Isabel Sawhill, the Brookings scholar who helped lead the work, "is that the ingrained expectation that our children are going to earn more than we do just doesn't hold true anymore for large numbers of Americans."

Exactly why this is happening isn't completely clear, but economists think one factor is the way technology is changing the nature of work. Through most of economic history, technical innovation displaced physical tasks—Pony Express riders gave way to the telegraph, secretaries gave way to voice mail. The automation of "thinking" jobs is a newer development. Not long ago, for example, people made good livings as mortgage underwriters, ruling on loan applications. Now such work is almost entirely computerized. The result is an increasingly polarized job market. Good jobs increasingly require expert thinking and complex communication; getting them increasingly depends on a good education. Jobs that don't include these tasks won't pay a decent wage.

Making matters worse, the new downward mobility findings come on the heels of recent international comparisons of upward mobility that would leave Abraham Lincoln and Ben Franklin aghast. The United States now offers its citizens a smaller chance of rising from their economic status at birth than do France, Denmark,

Norway, Sweden, Canada, and Germany. The contrast with the "good old days" is stark. After World War II, about one-fourth of the men whose fathers had been in the bottom quarter of the income distribution made it to the top quarter of income earners over their working lives. Now the figure is more like 6 percent. Thomas Piketty, an economist who has documented the extraordinary gains now going to the very top, frets that on our current path, "a small group of wealthy but untalented children will one day control vast segments of the U.S. economy, and penniless, talented children won't be able to compete."

What's even more worrying is that today's growing downward mobility has emerged *before* the full impact of global economic integration has been felt. Despite all the alarms about the rise of China and India, only an estimated 3.3 million jobs will be lost to offshoring by 2015—a tiny number over that period in an economy that boasts 147 million jobs and which created 1.7 million net new jobs last year. The real challenge will come in the following decades, and the risk isn't that jobs will actually disappear. It's that the presence of hungry, educated new workers, including many with comparable (or better) skills who will work for a fraction of what Americans expect to be paid, will put effective earnings caps on many American jobs. The International Monetary Fund estimates that the labor force available to global producers quadrupled from 1980 to 2005, with most of the increase coming in recent years. Princeton's Alan Blinder says up to 40 million U.S. jobs could be affected in the next two decades; he's already seen evidence that the wages paid for offshorable jobs are taking a hit. With 3 billion new capitalists entering the global workforce, he's probably on to something.

But the fact that many Americans will earn less than their parents does not mean the end of the good life in the United States. People will still have every chance to lead materially blessed and satisfying lives. Still, research and common sense tell us that people's attitudes and happiness are largely a function of their expectations, which are in turn shaped mostly by how they see their situation relative to what it was earlier in their lives, and compared to the experience of others they view as a reference point. It may be little solace to be reminded that you're living like kings compared to people who lived a hundred years ago, or compared to poor souls struggling in abject poverty in the Third World today.

From a global point of view, of course, the demise of the American Dream is hardly a tragedy. The economic change now hurting many relatively well-off Americans is helping myriad others in the poorer countries of the world. The rise of developing nations is a fantastic thing for humanity. Hundreds of millions of people have already been lifted from poverty, and literally billions more may follow. Science and technology continue to bring wondrous improvements and choices to every corner of life, even if these dynamics tend to sap the wages of people with fewer skills. But for those Americans hurt by these changes, a global point of view is cold comfort indeed.

WHICH WAY NOW?

So what will these new circumstances mean for individuals and the country? The answer will turn on how the new downward mobility affects Americans' attitudes toward the role of government. Public opinion surveys have long shown that Americans see themselves as authors of their economic fate, while Europeans tend to believe that forces outside the individual's control have greater influence. This helps explain why the United States has always had a smaller government than its European counterparts. In other nations, the first welfare innovations came from aristocrats and conservatives, like Otto von Bismarck in Germany or Benjamin Disraeli in Great Britain, who were comfortable with strong central authority; they introduced welfare provisions partly from a sense of obligation, and partly from a desire to protect their class's privileged position by keeping a lid on public anxiety amid economic change. The more meritocratic, market-oriented, and anti-statist United States didn't have the same dynamics, which is why it literally took a depression to get the enactment of the first modest version of Social Security.

Yet the forces that are now undermining upward mobility and generational advance in America are in fact largely outside people's control. Economists speak of the "skill-bias" of technological change making it harder for less educated workers to earn wages that can support a family. If you're a fifty-year-old autoworker who didn't go to college when that wasn't a prerequisite for a middle-class job, it's hard to fault you now for not having gotten more schooling then. The cost of health care, housing, and college have all risen much faster than incomes—what could any individual worker have done to stop that? Likewise, the rise of China and India was not affected by anything anyone did in Peoria; it's part of a historic adjustment in the world's economic activity. With so many outside forces now shaping our economic fate, is America's fierce optimism about the power of the individual sustainable? If not, does that mean Americans will be open to more aggressive policies (to bolster health care, pensions, and education, for example) that might promote economic opportunity and security, even if they mean higher taxes or "bigger government"? Democrats believe the answer is yes, but they're not confident enough about evolving sentiment to feel safe talking honestly about such choices. Republicans are convinced that the answer is no, and that their traditional assertion that government and taxes are "the problem" will remain effective. As the post–American Dream era unfolds, it's hard to imagine that the growing disconnect between the economic trajectory of millions of families and the nostalgia of our public debate can be sustained much longer.

Unfortunately, a more honest debate is no guarantee of a happy outcome. The longer we go through a period of income stagnation, the more people lose faith in the notion of progress. When incomes rise broadly, as they have for most of our history, upward mobility is celebrated and admired; when median incomes stagnate, and one person's gain comes at another's expense, upward mobility is resented. Our sunny optimism fades. Attitudes can turn bitter.

The political implication is that if we're facing a long period of downward mobility for much of the population, people will feel less generous. Politics will thus be less inclusive and magnanimous, making it less likely that we will coalesce around an agenda that eases the pain and expands opportunity, and more likely that we will vent at scapegoats. Benjamin Friedman, an economist at Harvard University and the author of *The Moral Consequences of Economic Growth,* sees this dynamic at work throughout American history. In periods of stagnation, such as the 1890s or today, we see a surge in anti-immigrant fervor, for example; only in periods of growth do we enact reforms meant to broaden security and opportunity, as we did in the Progressive Era and during the Great Society of the 1960s. Friedman acknowledges that the Depression is the great exception to this pattern, when the economic crisis was so severe it generated a sense of unity and political consensus for important new social initiatives.

If you're trying to be hopeful, Friedman's thesis poses a problem. Lenin famously argued "the worse, the better," meaning that deteriorating conditions for ordinary people under the tsars would hasten the revolution. Yet even as more of our children earn less than we do, it's not going to amount to anything like another Great Depression. It may be depressing, but that's not the same thing. The risk, therefore, if income stagnation does in fact act as a drag on social progress, is that we get stuck in a bad place—with too many of us losing ground in the face of large economic forces, but too few of us able to muster the collective will to improve our condition.

But there is another, more optimistic scenario: the pressure of events, though far short of a calamity like the Depression, forces America to tackle these questions anew. And the comforting news, at least from history's perspective, is that our challenge may in some sense be temporary. Britain, after all, was said to be in "decline" from the 1870s onward, even as living standards for the British rose massively over the ensuing hundred years. Many British families were hurt in those early decades when Britain lost its relative economic edge, but once a new global equilibrium had been reached, the broad British earnings escalator resumed its ascent. Similarly, a period of painful adjustment now for millions of Americans as other powers rise and new technologies are deployed throughout the economy is not inconsistent with an eventual return to broadly shared long-term increases in our material well-being. In other words, "the kids will earn more than we do" is a Dead Idea that could come back to life later in this century.

The critical question is how we define, or redefine, our obligations to those Americans who are fated to lose out during what may well be several decades of difficult transition. And that's a task that starts, first and foremost, inside our heads. There has never been a nation with so much of its self-image riding on the idea that the kids will earn more than we do. The death of this idea as the measure of American progress will force us to rebalance American capitalism, to augment our romance with the power of free men and free markets with a deeper awareness of its limits. Psychologists say that narcissists obsessed with their own "specialness" can be cured only when they learn to accept their ordinary humanity. Something like this acceptance in the realm of economic life lies ahead for the United States. We can't control every aspect of our economic trajectory in this new era, and the old inherited magic won't see all of us through. But we can control how we think about what is happening—and, more importantly, what we do about it.

2

FREE TRADE IS "GOOD"
(NO MATTER HOW MANY PEOPLE GET HURT)

*In which we discover that economists have been secretly playing
politics and hyping the case for trade in order to help
poor people around the world, even if it means misery at home*

In January 2008, Ralph Gomory, a retired seventy-eight-year-old
scientist with an idea, traveled from his home in Chappaqua, New
York, to Scottsdale, Arizona, to persuade 150 steel tubing executives that they'd been thinking about the world the wrong way. For
Gomory, it was a journey that really began in the 1980s, when, as
head of IBM's research division, a post he held for eighteen years,
he visited Japan often, in part to negotiate technology licensing
agreements with companies like Hitachi and Fujitsu. Gomory
came away stunned at how fast the Japanese were using American
know-how to catch up in computers and semiconductors. "It was
clear that from nowhere they were emerging as serious competitors with lots of government assistance," he recalled, "and that it
was going to be tough for IBM." At the time, he said, all the economists said this process was good for America—yes, there might be
some short-term pain as we adjusted to the kind of work these rising countries could do, but in the long run everyone would benefit.

Gomory felt certain this was wrong. He had long been troubled by the way economics as an academic discipline seemed out of touch with the realities he saw in global business. He promised himself he'd delve into the matter when he reached IBM's mandatory retirement age of sixty. And so he did. After Gomory left "Big Blue" and became president of the Sloan Foundation, updating the theory of free trade became his avocation. Gomory believed the ceding of U.S. industrial advantage he'd seen in Japan was poised to repeat itself on a larger scale with countries like India and China, and he was baffled that American economists were so in thrall to the benefits of trade that the country was mounting no strategy in response. Gomory knew he needed a card-carrying economist alongside him if he were to take on the profession's most sacred cow, so he hooked up with his old friend William Baumol of New York University, now eighty-six, among the most respected scholars in the field. The two went to work and published an academic volume in 2000, *Global Trade and Conflicting National Interests*, which explained why even the standard economic models showed it was perfectly possible for trade with developing economies to leave a country like the United States worse off. The book got polite reviews but was generally ignored. Meanwhile, Gomory's worries grew about the disconnect between what economists assured us about trade and what he saw happening. So did the public's anxiety, as evidenced by wide majorities who told pollsters in 2008 that they thought globalization was bad for the U.S. economy.

Which explains how Gomory, a mild-mannered grandfather wielding a PowerPoint, came to be in Scottsdale. It was part of his campaign—more than most of us might care to wage at age seventy-eight—to persuade businesspeople, public officials, and anyone else willing to listen that the received wisdom on globalization is hurting the country. The stakes, as he sees it, are nothing less than the survival of the American economy as we know it. "I hate to see our country headed for this disaster out of ignorance," Gomory told me, "pursuing policies based on a misconception" about the potential price of free trade. Gomory speaks to corporate boards, testifies before Congress, and writes op-eds. He's hardly a wild-eyed radical; indeed, with his quiet intelligence and affable demeanor, it's difficult to imagine a more reasonable advocate. Citing Gomory's impeccable business credentials, the trade critic William Greider wrote in *The Nation* that "the church of free trade . . . may have finally met its Martin Luther." "There's enormous resistance within the economics profession to the sort of thing we're saying," Gomory told me. "They really would rather it would go away—it doesn't fit with their notion that 'all is for the best in the best of all possible worlds.'"

Gomory is one of the few hardy souls taking on the trade establishment. But he's not alone. Alan Blinder of Princeton, President Clinton's former economic adviser, fired a salvo at his colleagues in 2006 with an article in *Foreign Affairs* entitled "Offshoring: The Next Industrial Revolution," in which he argued that communications and information technology have so transformed where work can be performed that tens of millions of U.S. jobs are now vulnerable, and policy makers must think anew. Economists have been firing back at Blinder ever since. Together, Gomory and Blinder represent the earliest mainstream challenges to a conception of trade whose obsolescence will become increasingly clear in the decade ahead.

They also bring us to the heart of what may be the most nuanced Dead Idea, because neither Gomory nor Blinder thinks protectionism is the answer. (Both agree it would make us worse off.) At first blush it may seem strange to say that the virtue of free trade is an idea whose "deadness" needs exposing. After all, there have always been passionate foes of free trade: the firms and workers who are directly hurt by foreign competition. But, despite periodic political victories, protectionists in the modern era have never been able to establish their framework as a serious rival to establishment thinking. Instead, they've been viewed as special pleaders. But what happens to the orthodox view of trade's benefits when the dissenters are credible and disinterested voices?

The question comes down to this: Why do we think free trade is the best policy when it can devastate industries and communities, and when the United States itself grew into the world's dominant economic power thanks to 150 years of protectionism? The answer is that economists have successfully persuaded America's leadership class that free trade is good for the country *no matter how many people get hurt,* and that today's globalization is just another form of free trade. There's only one problem: as a matter of economic science, these assertions are wrong. They are political judgments being peddled to the public under a patina of objective analysis. And the high priests of free trade know it. Economists, as we'll see, are a little like Colonel Nathan Jessup, the character played by Jack Nicholson in the film *A Few Good Men.* They don't think we can handle the truth about the downside of trade, and they hype their case to promote a hidden political agenda that mostly benefits people outside the United States. If this "vast economists' conspiracy" sounds treacherous, however, it's important to acknowledge that the treachery is well-meaning, because while economists have been wrong to mislead us, they've done so to save us from our darkest xenophobic impulses. This takes a bit of explaining, but the conclusion it points to is clear. The right way to move past the Dead Idea about trade isn't to return to protectionism—but rather to get serious about new protections for those Americans damaged by the tides of economic change, and for the federal government finally to pursue the strategy other nations follow as a matter of course: aggressively courting corporations and entrepreneurs to locate high value, high wage jobs here at home.

ADAM'S BIG IDEA

The idea of trade has been controversial since the dawn of civilization. The Greeks and Romans were elitists: they thought people from other lands were dirty barbarians, so it was best to have as little contact with them as possible. The medieval Christian scholastics, like St. Thomas Aquinas, fretted that such commerce bred greed and an unholy obsession with earthly goods. The seventeenth and eighteenth centuries saw the emergence of pamphleteers, many of them British merchants, who argued that the state needed to manipulate and manage trade for the good of the nation (not to mention their particular companies). Under Robert Walpole, the first British prime minister, Britain from the 1720s protected and subsidized manufacturing exporters under what was known as the "mercantilist system." Up to this point there was little discussion of, much less a systematic way of thinking about, the benefits of trade for average individuals and for society as a whole.

Then came Adam Smith, whose *Inquiry into the Nature and Causes of the Wealth of Nations* in 1776 is justly seen as a seminal breakthrough in the history of economic thought. Smith made a compelling case for free markets and free trade that remains relevant to this day. The division of labor allows people to develop special skills, Smith said. This specialization, coupled with the ability to trade freely, allows society to allocate resources most efficiently and maximize its income. Larger trading areas allow firms and individuals to specialize further and get better at what they do. Imagine a village that can support only one grocery store, for example. A larger village might have two or three. A bigger town will support more, some of which might focus on meats, others of which might specialize in fruits and vegetables. A bigger city will have enough customers to specialize even further—with some stores selling only pasta, others wine, still others cheeses. Before long you have everything from Wal-Mart to Whole Foods to the farmers' market. As Smith saw, bigger markets boost the efficiency of each producer and the choices available to consumers. You can't move from self-sufficiency to wealth-creating specialization without trade. And trade with other countries, Smith explained, is simply an extension of trade domestically: it increases society's wealth via the same mechanisms.

Smith's achievement was to be the first to fully appreciate and articulate this powerful economic logic, and to observe that competitive markets deliver these gains to society without any planning by distant authorities. Instead, the benefits emerge from the pursuit of self-interest, as if orchestrated by an "invisible hand." Virtually everything said on trade since Smith has been embellishment. Some forty years later, for example, David Ricardo added the idea of comparative advantage. Before Ricardo, people tended to think foreign trade held benefits only when a country could produce something more cheaply than its trading partners. Ricardo showed that people's intuition on this score was wrong: even when one country is less efficient at producing everything than another, it can gain by specializing in the thing in which it has the least cost disadvantage (while the efficient country gains by focusing on the thing in which it has the greatest cost advantage). Specializing in the goods or services where you are relatively better, and then trading, produces gains on all sides. As we'll see shortly, it's important to underscore that these classic arguments for the gains from trade are based on *efficiency*. The question Smith, Ricardo, and subsequent trade theorists essentially ask is, "What is the most efficient way to utilize a certain amount of resources in an open economy?" The answer is that everyone should specialize along the lines of their comparative advantage.

The Wealth of Nations made Smith internationally famous. Yet his insights, which revolutionized economic thinking, were ignored in his own country for decades. Smith passionately argued that mercantilist restrictions on competition via protectionism and subsidies were bad for the British economy, even if they helped certain firms. But well-placed commercial interests thought otherwise, so Britain didn't adopt free trade as a policy until the middle of the nineteenth century.

DO WHAT WE SAY, NOT WHAT WE DID

Across the Atlantic, Alexander Hamilton wasn't impressed with Smith's case either. Indeed, a dilemma for anyone trying to make sense of modern American thinking on trade is a forgotten paradox: the nation that is today the chief champion of open global markets got rich by practicing the opposite of what it now preaches. This was Hamilton's doing. Hamilton believed that manufacturing was indispensable to the growth of American wealth and power, and he argued that government protection and subsidies were needed to build manufacturing might. In his *Report on the Subject of Manufactures* in 1791, Hamilton rejected the counsel of the world's most famous economist and laid out his own blueprint for protecting "industries in their infancy" until they were sufficiently advanced to thrive against mature competitors abroad. In time, Hamilton's view became U.S. policy. Industrial tariffs rose from an average of 5 percent at the time Hamilton filed his report to 12.5 percent thereafter, then to 25 percent when the War of 1812 began, and to 40 percent by 1820. If the United States had spurned Hamilton's vision in favor of his rival Thomas Jefferson's ideal of an agrarian economy based on small independent farmers, we would never have grown into the world's greatest economic power. Abraham Lincoln was likewise a career-long champion of manufacturing, who endorsed the so-called American system of high protective tariffs and infrastructure investments. As president, Lincoln raised tariffs to their highest level to that point (partly to finance the Civil War), and they remained in the range of 40 to 50 percent until World War I. Average tariffs stabilized around 37 percent in the late 1920s, before the notorious Smoot-Hawley Act lifted average tariffs to 48 percent in 1930.

Modern economists tend to forget that the United States was not only the world's most protectionist economy during this period but also the fastest growing. It was only after World War II that the United States, by then the predominant industrial power, shifted gears and began to champion the cause of free trade, much as Britain had done when its industries were on top. This choice was in large measure a reaction to the global depression of the 1930s, which was seen to have been perversely deepened and prolonged by the decade's tariff wars, thus contributing to the rise of fascism. In the wake of World War II's unprecedented devastation, the leaders of the victorious Allied powers sought to diminish international tensions and rivalries; expanded commerce was central to their strategy. That American industry was by this time poised to benefit enormously from an expansion of global trade (largely because European and Japanese industries had been decimated) made this direction supremely attractive to U.S. policy makers. This linkage between security goals and economic advantage led the United States to reduce average tariffs to around 10 percent by 1950.

Thanks to geopolitical imperatives, then, Adam Smith finally triumphed in American thinking. Implicit in this development was another radical change: economists were being seriously heeded for the first time. In 1930, a thousand economists had signed a public petition urging President Herbert Hoover not to approve the dread Smoot-Hawley tariff bill, but Hoover signed it anyway. Now economists were seen as having important insights to offer, and the postwar boom only bolstered the prestige of their ideas. Writing popular books and magazine articles when they weren't hobnobbing with politicians and business leaders, economists became the sexiest of the new social science intelligentsia, on whose mystical wisdom prosperity seemed to depend.

Of course, the virtue of free trade was perhaps the single most cherished insight in the economic canon. It was an idea that economists saw themselves nobly defending against the threat of protectionist barbarians bent on shutting down the system and the benefits it showered on all. Still, as Ralph Gomory sensed when globetrotting for IBM, something was seriously incomplete about the theory developed by Smith, Ricardo, and their progeny, even though it had captured the American economic mind.

GLOBALIZATION IS *NOT* FREE TRADE

Gomory's message before audiences like the one he spoke to in Scottsdale is simple: globalization is not the same as free trade, as most economists mistakenly insist. That's because the classic "gains from trade" are based on a premise that is not made explicit: they assume that *each country's productive capabilities are fixed*—that is, each country has a certain amount of labor, land, and capital, and they can put them all together, given their existing levels of technical ingenuity, to churn out certain widgets. The "gains from trade" flow from trade in the goods and services that those fixed capabilities provide. Everyone agrees that free trade in such circumstances, looked at as a kind of snapshot in time, raises the national income of both trading partners. To be fair, this was an important insight for economics to deliver, because powerful industrialists through the ages have wrongly insisted that protecting their enterprises is good for society overall, when it's really just good for their own bottom line. But if the assumption of fixed productive capacities seems like a weirdly unreal constraint, welcome to the world of economic reasoning.

When productive capabilities are not fixed, the situation changes. Raising productive capability—that is, getting better at producing things of value—is the obvious goal of developing countries, and it is also precisely the situation globalization makes possible, as technology and know-how move from advanced countries to less advanced countries, often via the actions of multinational firms. Gomory and Baumol make the argument that *globalization is* not *free trade—it is free trade* plus *productivity changes,* which they term "a whole new ball game." When the United States trades semiconductors for Asian T-shirts, that is trade in the old-fashioned sense, in which both countries plainly benefit. "But when U.S. companies build semiconductor plants and R&D facilities in Asia rather than in the U.S.," Gomory and Baumol write, "then that is a change in productive capacities . . . and there is nothing in either common sense or economic theory which says that improvement in the productive capabilities of other countries is necessarily good for your country."

Take India as another example, and imagine that U.S. firms build new high-end microchip factories there that use cutting-edge technologies. As India pursues this higher-value economic activity, its wages begin to rise. This has good and bad implications for the United States. On the plus side: a wealthier India becomes a better customer for our exports, and with rising wages, Indian workers pose less of a threat to the wages of our own labor force. On the downside, however, the goods we buy from India become more expensive, because wages and thus prices there are rising. And, perhaps most important, we risk the loss of the all-important microchip industry, in which we have an edge today. Bottom line: there is no guarantee that the net effect of these changes will be positive for the United States as a whole. Trade economists acknowledge that Gomory and Baumol's framework is correct; it actually builds on theories that have been quietly kicked around since at least the 1980s. But they're skeptical as to whether governments are competent enough to do anything about it. Gomory and Baumol's research suggests that the net impact of trade with developing countries tips to negative when the average wage of the country we're trading with rises to one-fourth or one-third of the average U.S. wage. The size of the trading partner also matters, they say; we get into losing territory earlier when the partner has a large population. Sound like any countries you know?

BELIEVING IS SEEING

Another point Gomory makes seems obvious but is widely ignored: under globalization, the interests of companies and of countries can now dramatically diverge. Offshoring jobs and know-how to developing countries is generally smart and profitable for American-based firms even if such moves ultimately hurt the United States. This tension between their fiduciary duty to share-holders and their broader loyalty as citizens makes American executives profoundly uncomfortable.

Ask Gomory how people react to his case as he makes the rounds, and you get a feel for the way human nature helps Dead Ideas persist. "What makes an argument believable to people, or attractive to people, is that they already believe it," he says.

> Another way of saying the same thing is: People easily believe what they want to believe, and it's exceedingly difficult to get people to believe things they don't want to believe. Our thesis about the impact of globalization, or about the inherent conflict now between nations and corporations, is a message that most economists don't wish to believe. The corporations engaged in this activity certainly do not wish to believe it. So the difficulty lies there, not in the arguments themselves. . . . The ones who like it are the ones who want to believe it. The ones who don't like it are the ones who don't want to believe it. It's impressive how strong that effect is.

Gomory finds that his audiences become frustrated as well. "I've heard very picturesque questions like: 'Okay, suppose what you say is true. What do you want us to do, bomb China back into the stone age because it's their growth that's hurting us?' I mean, there's a very emotional reaction, with people saying that you can't do anything about it. And that's dead wrong, because if you just look and see what the other countries are doing, they're all doing things to make this happen. It didn't just happen."

What Gomory means is that China, India, and just about every other ambitious developing country has a national economic strategy, and one of the chief aims of that strategy is to get major corporations to transfer new technologies to and locate high value jobs in their country. It's basically a deal: companies want profits, countries want GDP, and countries figure out how to strike a bargain that gives both sides what they seek. In the old days, profits and GDP mostly went together in America for U.S.-based firms; nowadays, profits are increasingly found elsewhere, and that is costing America some GDP. The obvious response, Gomory says, is to reward the kind of corporate behavior we want, and thus "realign the interests of companies with those of the country." Only in America is there a laissez-faire attitude toward this question. Gomory believes we should adjust corporate tax rates according to the value added by the workers of corporations operating in the United States. A company with high value added per U.S. employee would pay a low tax rate, and those with low value added per U.S. employee would pay a high rate. This would encourage companies with high value added jobs to locate their operations in the United States.

This proposal isn't a panacea. But it's a start. Once we get past our collective denial, we'll start the broader debate we need on the range of possible remedies. The first step is to change how we're thinking. As Gomory puts it, "It's a system problem, not an 'evil man' problem. I know this because I'm one of the evil men." As a member of the board of directors of Lexmark, a printer company spun off from IBM in 1995 that now has $5 billion in sales, he has supported moving production out of the United States to lower cost countries. "As a director I look out for the profits of the shareholders," he explains. "We need to change the system. At the moment there is no will. The government still treats the companies as if they represent the country, but they don't."

ARE "WE" "WINNING" YET?

Let's put to one side now these modern developments that call into question whether trade with developing countries will really be a "win-win" proposition in the era ahead. There's actually a deeper secret that economists have been keeping for two centuries. It turns out that economists have been practicing politics without a license when they claim that even their traditional models tell us free trade is "good" for the country.

How can that be? Basic trade theory notes that there will be winners and losers from trade. Textile workers in South Carolina lose their jobs when cheaper Chinese goods come in, for example, yet other Americans benefit from lower clothing prices. Smith, Ricardo, et al. showed that the amount the winners gain will be greater than the amount the losers lose. So far, so straightforward. But then comes the perilous leap. On what basis can economists say that the loss suffered by some Americans is "outweighed" by the gain reaped by other Americans, so that the net impact, as a matter of economic science, is certifiably "good" for the country?

"What most economists don't realize is that when they say that free trade is good for the country as a whole, they're adding an ethical layer almost unthinkingly," says Dani Rodrik, a leading trade iconoclast at the Harvard Kennedy School. "You're now taking off your hat as an economist and you're putting on your hat as a political philosopher."

As Rodrik points out, we wouldn't leap to this conclusion in any other context. "Suppose I didn't tell you that it was trade," he says.

But suppose I just went to you and said, "I'm going to take five dollars away from you and give six dollars to somebody else. And I want you to tell me whether it is a good thing or a bad thing." Nobody would be able to immediately jump to the conclusion, "Oh, it's got to be good because we've created one additional dollar." They'll want to ask questions. Who's losing, who's gaining? What's the mechanism through which this has occurred?

Compounding the uncertainty of what makes for "goodness" here is a fact that economists understand but rarely bother to explain: the distributional impact of trade can sometimes be bigger than its efficiency gains. That means that if some people (call them consumers) gain six dollars from trade, while others (call them unskilled workers) lose five dollars, the "efficiency gain" toted up by economists is one dollar. The losers thus suffer five times the net gain so that "we" "win" overall. With evidence like that, it's no surprise that the benefits of free trade look different from the unemployment line than they do from the ivory tower.

Rodrik's point is poorly understood, routinely overlooked, and indispensable: *gains from trade occur precisely via trade's distributional impact.* The bigger you think the economy-wide gains from trade are, in other words, the more pain you think is being inflicted on losers. Why is this the case? Because the mechanism through which trade creates gains is the restructuring of economic activity. In our example above, South Carolina's textile workers lose their jobs and find employment that pays less well elsewhere. People who shop at Wal-Mart and Target, meanwhile, benefit from new low prices available thanks to overseas supply. By implicitly valuing efficiency over distributional concerns in calling the results of trade "good" for all of us, economists have been peddling ideology under the guise of science. This isn't a matter of semantics but of genuine cultural power; there's no question that economics' tradition of labeling free trade "good for the country" has helped create the intellectual inertia with which Gomory, Blinder, and the rest of us now grapple.

As it turns out, inside the tribe, some economists have been uncomfortable with this sleight of hand for ages. Nassau Senior, a contemporary of David Ricardo, said that an economist might tell people how to increase their wealth (via measures like free trade, which he supported), but whether that meant a particular course was actually *advisable* was beyond the economist's ken. Senior wrote: "An author who, having stated that a given conduct is productive of Wealth, should, on that account alone, recommend it . . . would be guilty of the absurdity of implying that Happiness and the possession of Wealth are identical." A century later, Lionel Robbins, a giant of the profession at the London School of Economics, wrote a hotly debated manifesto in a similar spirit in the 1930s urging his colleagues to be clear about the limits of what economic science could offer. The power of economics was its ability to show that x or y would happen as the result of particular policy choices, Robbins explained. But to conclude that a policy was therefore good or bad required judgments from the realms of philosophy and politics. Robbins was perfectly happy for economists to enter the public debate on these questions, but he insisted they be honest about where economic science ended and personal advocacy began. This view rankled many of his colleagues, who desperately wanted economics to be a "real" science, like physics. After all, if economics as a science couldn't offer presidents and prime ministers firm conclusions about what to do, why would they ever want to talk to economists?

To solve this problem, economists cooked up something called "the compensation principle." Essentially they argued that because free trade created enough gains for the winners to be able to compensate the losers for their losses and still be better off themselves, economic science could conclude that free trade was indeed "good" for the country. But here's the catch: the compensation didn't actually have to occur. It just had to be theoretically possible! If unconvincing arguments like this are the best that economics can do, little wonder the profession's credibility is at risk. As Rodrik puts it: "The gains from trade do not become real unless and until there is compensation."

In the real world, of course, compensation for trade's losers almost never occurs. Trade adjustment assistance programs have always been tiny, poorly funded stepchildren. More general compensation schemes like "wage insurance" (to ease the pain for displaced workers who take lower paying jobs) have gotten little discussion beyond a handful of policy elites.

As a practical matter, the distributional consequences of free trade weren't as pressing an issue when the benefits of overall growth were more broadly shared in America. All economic boats were rising. But now, as we saw in chapter 1, with slow or no income growth for many Americans, this blind spot in economic thinking is costly and unacceptable. The entry of India, China, and the nations of the former Soviet Union into the global economy has doubled the supply of labor while adding little to the supply of capital. Any way you slice it, that's bad news for workers in wealthier countries. In this new context it is senseless to assert that free trade is "good" no matter how many people get hurt.

DON'T TELL THE KIDS

Which brings us to the heart of darkness, so to speak. The points we've just discussed about trade's distributional consequences are straightforward. Most economics professors will tell you that trade's inevitable creation of winners and losers is the second thing they teach, after first lecturing on comparative advantage and the gains from trade. So why don't economists acknowledge trade's downside more readily outside the seminar room? The answer has more to do with paternalism than with social science. Economists would really prefer that "the kids" (that is, we the people) didn't know about all this, because if we did, irresponsible barbarians might seize on these facts to push protectionist agendas that cascade into trade wars that harm the entire world, as happened in the

1930s. It's a slippery slope out there, and economists are keeping us in the dark for our own good.

"Of all the policy-relevant aspects of economics," says Alan Blinder, "the one on which there is the closest to total unanimity among economists is that free trade is good. The result is that anyone in the fraternity who says anything that could even obliquely give aid and comfort to the enemies of free trade is considered traitorous." Blinder should know. His articles and lectures about the threats posed by offshoring are prefaced by almost comically rehearsed vows of fealty to free trade, yet he is nonetheless skewered for his apostasy.

"We would be more successful as advocates in the political sphere if we were more honest about these issues," says Paul Romer, an economist at Stanford University whose pioneering work in growth theory has led some to speculate he will one day win the Nobel Prize.

> It may be well intentioned, but the stance we've been taking is to obfuscate what's going on here. I think people are starting to see through that stance and it's undermining our credibility and it calls into question our motivations. People ask, why are we being dishonest about this? I think both as scientists and as people who are trying to influence public policy, we really should stick to "know the truth and it will set you free." We shouldn't spend so much time trying to spin our message because we think we understand how the politics of it will play out.

WAIT A MINUTE!

If you're with me to this point, it's plain that we can't say free trade is "good" for the country unless the losers are actually compensated. But wait a minute. There's a problem for this whole line of argument. If we can't say trade is good without compensation, how can we say technological improvement is good? This would be troubling, because if economics can't say that, it would be as if the field has nothing to say at all, because technological improvement is indisputably what has given us our epic rise in living standards since the early nineteenth century. Yet there are always losers from new technologies. When Edison invented the lightbulb he put countless candle makers out of work. When Steve Jobs invented the iPod, traditional stereo manufacturers took a hit. Seen this way, trade is really just a subset of economic change viewed more broadly, and there are always losers from capitalism's "creative destruction." (That's why it's called "destruction.") It can't be right that losers always have to be compensated before we can say technological innovation is good. Can it? What does it mean for our explosion of the "trade is good" view if it bleeds into this broader question regarding economic change itself? Are there ways to distinguish how we think about trade from how we think about technology?

Alan Blinder thinks there are. Trade expansions are a matter of government action imposing this cost on some set of losers, he argues. By contrast, technological innovations are made by private individuals in the private economy; someone invents a better mousetrap and therefore displaces the people who made the old, inferior mousetrap. It wasn't the government that put the candle makers out of work, it was Thomas Edison. It wasn't the government that made secretaries redundant, it was the company's decision to put in a voice mail system. "There's a different onus or set of judgments economics can apply to something that is about a government policy choice," Blinder says. And in other cases where harmful things are visibly done by the government, we often compensate the losers, as when private property is taken for public purposes under the doctrine of eminent domain. "This distinction between what the government hath wrought and what nature hath wrought, or what anonymous markets hath wrought, is an important and operational one," Blinder adds.

That's not a bad try, but to my mind, it's unpersuasive. At an intellectual level, I don't believe you can distinguish trade and technological change in satisfying ways that would argue for compensation in one case but not in the other. The real difference is practical: people react to these two types of economic change very differently. The political resonance of damage done by trade is much bigger than it is for damage done by technology. There's no shame in saying that our system needs to treat these two cases differently; it's not called *political* economy for nothing. As Lincoln famously noted, "a universal feeling, whether well or ill-founded, cannot be safely disregarded." Especially by politicians. Americans point to a trade agreement with Mexico and say, "That caused these six factories in Illinois to shut down." When something is invented in Silicon Valley that leads to six factories in Illinois shutting down, people don't have the same sense of grievance. Not since the Luddites lost their fight against mechanized looms in England in the early nineteenth century has an antitechnology movement gotten serious traction.

FEAR OF FOREIGNER vs. FEAR OF GEEK

Why are people's intuitions and reactions so different in these two cases? It's hard to know for sure, but it's probably traceable to the "us versus them" mentality that seems baked into human nature, and which has had such bloody consequences for the world. People seem to feel it's one thing to have your job automated by a robot, and quite another to lose it to someone in China who makes two dollars a day. Technology feels like progress, while trade feels more like theft. We treat trade and technology differently, in other words, because we fear the foreigner more than we fear the geek. If we were rational, of course, we'd find the geek much scarier: far more of our economy's disruptive change comes from innovative technologies than from trade. But because we're not rational, because people have a darker, xenophobic side, those who want to see the world (especially the developing world) capture the gains from trade feel an extra duty to support it. *This is what economists are really up to. Their redeeming secret is that in hyping the case for free trade, and shielding us from the truth, their ultimate aim is to keep markets open enough for capitalism to work its magic and lift billions of desperate people from grinding poverty in the world's developing countries.* Yes, there are benefits to free trade for advanced nations like the United States—and yes, closing the borders would hurt all sides— but the biggest gains from trade at this juncture in history will go to poorer nations, who stand to benefit most as advanced technologies are dispersed.

"Are the gains from trade potentially large?" asks Paul Romer. "I think they're enormous. But they're allocated asymmetrically." He goes on:

> The big gains are going to come for the poorest people in the world. And the gains to the richest countries are modest, at best. And they, unfortunately, come in this very skewed form, where a few people, the most talented people who can benefit from this arbitrage of technology across regions, they do terrifically with it, but a bunch of other people in the U.S. suffer. This commitment to free trade for a lot of us comes from this real concern for the most disadvantaged people on earth, but it comes in this ambivalent way. Free trade is radically reducing inequality *between* nations. In that sense it's a very equalizing force in our lives right now, and if you care about the worst off people in the world, it is a terrifically beneficial thing. But unfortunately it's accompanied by increased inequality *within* nations. So ironically, worldwide inequality can

be going down dramatically, but everybody in every nation sees inequality going up, because they're looking at what they see nearby.

This desire most economists share for seeing trade and capitalism lift poorer nations shows why the clash between the new trade skeptics and the old trade purists has been utterly misconstrued by the press. It's not a showdown between protectionism and free trade, as the media suggest. It's a dispute about which *tactics* can best assure that we have no protectionist backlash in wealthy nations that ultimately hurts the world's poor. The purists act as if we can't let the kids know about the losers from trade, or people will misuse that knowledge and we'll be on our way down the slippery slope. Skeptics say the kids already know; we've hardly been able to stop the losers from seeing that they're losing! That's why polls show that Americans of all education and skill levels now think globalization is bad for the U.S. economy, a dramatic change from a decade ago. We need to acknowledge the obvious, skeptics say, and get serious about new forms of economic security that will keep this anxiety from spawning a revolt against open markets altogether.

FROM PROTECTIONISM TO "PROTECTIONS"

In the end, this idea of enhanced security in the face of economic change is the response that both free trade and technological innovation should push us to embrace. Instead of direct compensation of losers per se, we should think of this as a new brand of "protection" that fends off protectionism by assuring a decent society. Trade purists always say they support this agenda, but they treat it as a throwaway line. In the era ahead it must become the first, second, and third thing out of their mouths, not an afterthought. Today's prevailing idea, that "free trade is good no matter how many people get hurt," should yield to a new formulation: that free trade is good, *provided we have protections in place to make people feel sufficiently secure in a time of rapid economic change.* This means health care and pension security that aren't tied to a job that can suddenly disappear. It means broader trade adjustment assistance, job retraining, and wage insurance that keeps offshoring from being a catastrophe for affected families. It also means politicians with the gumption and creativity to put this agenda at the center of public debate by saying that we should not be expanding trade further until we have these protections in place. The new rallying cry might be: "No major trade deals until everyone has the same health care plan as every member of Congress."

Wealthy nations whose markets are more integrated with the world's are way ahead of us on this score. It's no accident that countries with higher exports and imports than ours compared to the size of their economy—as in Europe and Scandinavia—have higher levels of taxes and spending as a share of GDP as well. Social insurance is the flip side of the open economy.

When I was in law school in the mid-1980s, I studied property law under a professor who epitomized the way economists have come to warp the American mind on these matters. Whenever a student questioned the fairness of some decision under review, or challenged a policy that seemed to leave millions with few resources and little hope, his response was the same. He'd open his palms skyward in a gesture that mingled helplessness with contempt, and declaim in a thick Eastern European accent: *"Poverty? That's purely a distributive question."* Manly economists don't redistribute income, he was saying; they boost economic growth. The sissies can come in afterward and worry about who gets what. This way of thinking is about to go the way of the dinosaur. It won't let us preserve a political consensus for the trade and economic change that in the long run does benefit us all, even as it inflicts real pain on many of us right now. In an anxious era, "real men" redistribute.

. . .

It's a lesson that business in particular needs to learn. During the 2006 midterm election campaign, Rahm Emanuel, the brash Illinois congressman who helped Democrats sweep the House that year, met with the officers of the Business Roundtable. The Roundtable is Washington's premier CEO lobby, representing 160 companies with $4.5 trillion in revenues and 10 million employees. Over lunch in the organization's Washington office, the chief executives of some of the largest companies in the country told Emanuel that the biggest threat to U.S. prosperity was rising protectionist sentiment, particularly among Democrats. How can further trade expansion be assured, they asked, when CAFTA, the Central American Free Trade Agreement—a relatively modest deal, after all, with a handful of small countries—passed by a whisker, and with just fifteen Democratic votes in the House? Emanuel set down his fork and looked at the executives around the table. "You've got an economic problem?" he said. "Well, I've got a political problem. Unless you make my people feel more secure, you're not going to pass another trade agreement here in our lifetime."

The dilemma, as we're about to see, is that business plays an inappropriately central role in providing this security.

3

YOUR COMPANY SHOULD
TAKE CARE OF YOU

In which we find that an employer-based benefits system
designed to beat back communism is now strangling business
and stranding workers in an age of global competition

We begin with three scenes of corporate cognitive dissonance:

SCENE 1: Rick Wagoner, the CEO of General Motors, joins the
CEOs of Chrysler and Ford to meet with President George W. Bush
in the Oval Office to discuss the industry's competitive challenges.
Health care tops their agenda. The Big Three have reported billions
in losses that they attribute partly to soaring health care expenses,
costs that now exceed $1,500 per car. As a result, Detroit has slashed
tens of thousands of jobs. The executives explain to the president
that foreign automakers have a huge advantage, because their governments cover most employee and retiree health care expenses.
Then Wagoner tells the president the same thing he's said to groups
around the country. "I want to be clear," he says, "I'm not saying we
expect the government to pick these expenses up."

SCENE 2: Union leaders representing thousands of workers at one
of America's best-known companies ask the firm to look at an

interesting question. What would the impact be on profits and shareholder value, they ask, if national reforms were adopted that assured health coverage for every American while permanently *lowering* the amount the company contributed to such benefits? The company does the analysis, and a top executive calls the union with the news.

"We looked at what you suggested," he says, "and the impact is huge."

"Great," says the union leader. "We'd love to review it with you."

"I'm afraid we're not comfortable sharing it," says the executive.

"What do you mean?" the union official says. "Why not?"

The executive pauses.

"Because the numbers are so big you'd never understand why we won't want to pursue this as a matter of policy."

SCENE 3:   Steve Burd, the CEO of Safeway, is arguably the most passionate and involved business leader working on the health care crisis today. The wellness and financial incentives that Burd has incorporated into Safeway's health care plan may well become a model for improving health while trimming costs. He's the force behind a business coalition advocating reforms that would achieve universal coverage in market-friendly ways. Yet when I ask him why business should be in this business in the first place—why corporate America should carry so much of the national health care tab and administrative burden on its payroll—he is adamant. "I want to make sure that you don't think that we, or anybody else in our coalition, is interested in turning this thing over to somebody else," he says. "We're not."

The American business mind is in the grip of a Dead Idea. It's an idea that was born a century ago, when industrial capitalism's brutality and insecurity first sparked a political convulsion in the

United States. This idea has become so ingrained in our collective psyche that it serves as a kind of wallpaper in our economic life, always present but rarely articulated. Once uttered aloud, however, this premise feels jarring and peculiar, and ultimately hard to defend. It runs as follows: if people need to reach beyond family to achieve a measure of security against life's major risks (such as ill health or poverty in old age), *they should look to their employer, not their country, for support.*

The United States is unique among advanced nations in organizing much of its society around this notion, and in building a vast array of institutions that cement its primacy in our culture. What has been forgotten, however, is that these exceptional arrangements, under which business became responsible for much of our health care, retirement, and other forms of social provision, took root in a specific historical context. The story usually told about how this happened is misleading. During World War II, the conventional account runs, when wages and prices were legally frozen, offering benefits (not subject to the freeze) became a way for employers to compete for talent. After the war the federal government enacted new tax subsidies that encouraged this practice, and it exploded. This "explanation" is true so far as it goes, but it makes it sound as if our massive (and poorly understood) corporate welfare state was created by accident, as a mere by-product of wartime economic policy.

This obscures the richer, more important story that dates to the backlash against capitalism in the early twentieth century, when business and its conservative political allies were desperate for a way to tamp down labor unrest (and stave off "the revolution") without putting America on the road to socialism being trod elsewhere. Placing the onus on employers, not government, to provide various forms of welfare became the strategy. The employer-based model subsequently thrived thanks to a decisive historical fluke: the unprecedented position the U.S. economy held after World War II.

With the world in tatters, and little foreign competition, it was easy for corporate America to pass on, via higher prices, the costs of much of the country's safety net. But today, because of transformations in the way we live and the way the global economy works, this organizing idea leaves tens of millions of Americans vulnerable and anxious, while shackling companies with soaring costs that render them uncompetitive.

Seen this way, our inherited view of the corporation's role in America's welfare state is a relic of the Cold War—a tool in our long national effort to triumph over communism. But that war ended twenty years ago. The global economy has transformed the context. Despite what some critics said as the government moved to rescue the financial sector in 2008, the risk of America's becoming socialist is now approximately zero, but the risk that worker anxiety will lead America to become protectionist is profound and real. Yet American business hasn't rethought its role, even as it now spends more on health care than it earns in profits. Remarkably, many prominent executives and Republican politicians believe this employer-based system shouldn't change much, while Democrats typically think companies should be forced to do even more. The path beyond an idea that no longer serves the interest of business or the nation starts with the largely untold story of how we came to do things this way in the first place. As we'll see, the huge "legacy costs" decried by business leaders today aren't the legacy of "greedy unions" at all—they're the legacy of a successful corporate strategy to fend off a larger public role in providing economic security for ordinary Americans.

THE WAGES OF FEAR

Deep into the nineteenth century, when much of the American economy still resembled the Jeffersonian ideal of the yeoman farmer, there were no such things as job-related "benefits." Your job *was* your benefit. But after the Civil War, when a traumatized nation enacted pensions for indigent veterans, widows, and dependents, the idea of support for those no longer able to work entered the culture. In the private sector it was picked up first by the railroads, the industrial behemoths of the time. Pensions became a way to ease aging, less productive workers out the door without simply firing them, which, besides being cruel, was demoralizing to those who remained. The railroads and other giant firms also came to see pensions as a way to retain skilled workers over a career.

Up to the Depression, pensions were the most prevalent financial benefit companies offered. But in those same years, from 1890 to 1930, a slew of other benefits started to appear at such large progressive firms as Procter & Gamble, General Electric, National Cash Register, S. C. Johnson & Son, Denison Manufacturing, and Filene's Department Stores. These new programs ran the gamut from employer-provided housing, recreation, and educational programs to lunchrooms, paid vacations, mortgage assistance, and workplace health and safety initiatives. The employer acted almost as a feudal lord, paternalistically overseeing his subjects. Though these benefits never came to serve a broad segment of American workers, the movement known as "welfare capitalism" captured the imagination of big business, academia, and the press.

Some firms introduced these benefits to help recruit and retain workers. Others did so out of a sense of moral or patriotic duty, convinced that they should help "Americanize" their immigrant workforces, using the company town to shape workers' lives. Still others were sold on these ideas by insurance companies, which saw a potential gold mine in peddling pensions and accident insurance (an early version of health coverage) to big firms.

But the broader context for all this activity was fear. The 1880s and 1890s had seen strikes turn violent at companies like Pullman and Homestead Steel. The Industrial Workers of the World, led by

"Big Bill" Haywood, was rumored to be behind a number of bomb-
ings and other industrial disruptions. The Socialist presidential candidate Eugene V. Debs went from getting fewer than a hundred
thousand votes in 1900 to a million in 1912, while Socialist Party
members won election to a thousand state and local offices. Meanwhile, in Europe, new labor-based political parties were agitating
for governments to soften the harsh edges of industrial life.

Though it was little noted at the time, business's drive to co-opt
workers and fend off government was largely underwritten by
monopoly profits. Firms in industries such as steel, automobiles,
railroads, copper, petroleum, and business machines became
nationally integrated between 1900 and 1920. The dread era of "cut-
throat competition" gave way to "price maintenance" and stable,
outsized profit margins. This made it easy for the big progressive
employers to pay higher wages and benefits. With their dominant
positions cemented by sky-high tariffs that were then a centerpiece
of U.S. economic policy, the cost of welfare capitalism was passed
on to consumers.

Unions, meanwhile, were happy to let American business take
the lead. Though it may seem surprising today, in the early twentieth century, unions were deeply mistrustful of government. The
state, in their view, was the reactionary police power that broke
strikes. It was the pro-business courts that threw out minimum
wage and safety laws. Moreover, as Samuel Gompers of the American Federation of Labor believed, if the state got into the business
of providing benefits, it would undercut workers' loyalty to their
unions. This helps to explain why Gompers was a key foe of government efforts to pass compulsory health insurance programs
modeled on the system Bismarck had introduced in Germany in
the 1880s.

At industrial capitalism's first major inflection point, then, history was unfolding very differently in America. This mystified
Europeans at the time. In 1905, Warner Sombart, a German econ-

omist, wrote a famous essay whose title asked the question on every continental leftist's mind: "Why Is There No Socialism in the United States?" Though there were fancier sociological reasons, Sombert's bottom line was *rising prosperity*. American socialism, he memorably wrote, had foundered "on the reefs of roast beef and apple pie"—a hefty helping of which had been served up by business with that very aim.

MARION'S WAY

Then came the Depression, and the bottom fell out. Companies went bust, laying off workers by the millions. Pensions and other welfare programs were shut down as firms struggled to survive. American business lay discredited. Almost overnight, the idea that companies could provide security in the face of modern capitalism's turbulence seemed untenable. Crusaders like Dr. Francis Townsend led growing movements to have government provide universal pensions and unemployment insurance, fanning pressures to which Franklin D. Roosevelt wished, and felt compelled, to respond. To the horror of many business executives, a transformative expansion of the American state seemed imminent. At this juncture an unusual business leader emerged whose career both symbolized and shaped business's shrewd accommodation to these new social realities while preserving the primacy of the private sector's role in responding to them.

Marion Folsom was born in Georgia in 1893 and attended Harvard Business School on the eve of World War I, at a time when two precepts were dominant. The first was the technocratic belief that all problems, industrial or social, were amenable to solution by educated, dispassionate professionals. The second was that gifted young men had social obligations to the nation. A slim, mild-mannered man who the press later said had the demeanor of an actuary or "a benevolent principal of an old-fashioned small town high school," Folsom caught the eye of the legendary film and photo entrepreneur George Eastman, and he went to work for Eastman Kodak as the founder's "statistical secretary" after his graduation from Harvard in 1914. He rose to the company's top ranks, where he remained, with breaks for several government stints, for half a century.

It was in Rochester, where Kodak was based, that Folsom first became fascinated by questions of social welfare. The city was hit hard by the postwar slump of 1920–21, and Eastman, its leading citizen, felt he should do something. By chance Folsom had heard B. Seebohm Rowntree, the progressive British employer and philanthropist, give a lecture on unemployment insurance, which had recently been introduced in Britain; in Rowntree's view it had spared the country from "something like a revolution." Folsom knew Eastman had been spooked by widespread strikes in Rochester the year before. Advising his boss that "fear of unemployment is one of the most potent causes of labor unrest," Folsom pitched the idea of Kodak's setting up its own unemployment plan, and the old man gave the okay. The idea was shelved when the economy recovered, but Folsom had gotten the bug. He traveled to Europe to examine its emerging social insurance program, and he boned up on pensions. By 1929, when Folsom persuaded Eastman to launch Kodak's innovative pension plan, it was viewed as such a striking advance that the prestigious *Atlantic Monthly* magazine asked Folsom to write a long essay about it. When the Depression hit, Folsom dusted off his unemployment plan, got a dozen other firms in town to join, and in 1931 announced the launch of the privately run Rochester Unemployment Benefit Fund, which paid 60 percent of salary to unemployed workers for thirteen weeks. This novel corporate attempt to address the crisis vaulted Folsom to national prominence. Business groups across the country asked him to speak. Franklin D. Roosevelt, then the governor of New York, sought his counsel. Yet even as he proselytized for Kodak's approach, Folsom's own outlook was evolving. He had initially hoped that other firms would emulate what Kodak had pioneered, but he gradually saw that the scale of the need presented by a calamity like the Depression required the government to act. Roosevelt recruited Folsom in 1933 to serve as one of a handful of progressive business advisers to his Committee for Economic Security, charged with drafting the plans for what became Social Security and unemployment insurance.

"He saw the handwriting on the wall," says Sanford Jacoby, the author of the definitive study of Folsom's career. "It was inevitable that the United States was going to move in a European direction. And he basically said, rather than try to beat them, we might as well join them, become an insider, try to influence the evolution of the legislation so that an employer role is preserved. He was always looking for what we would today call 'win-win solutions' that kept a role for the private sector while also recognizing that the private sector couldn't do it all on its own."

Folsom envisioned a minimal welfare state supplemented by employer-provided benefits. In Social Security, that meant keeping the benefit small enough that employers would have a rationale, and an incentive, to build on it with pensions of their own. Folsom was one of the few business leaders who openly supported Social Security, arguing that it would serve as a stabilizing force and that it was better than more radical options being discussed. Once businessmen got past their ideological blinders, Folsom argued, they would see that they would actually gain from the new Social Security plan, because it would let big firms *shrink* their own retirement offerings, allowing the combined government and private plans to give workers the same total benefit. The program would impose new costs on low-priced competitors (via payroll taxes) and thus help level the playing field with firms who until this point had not offered workers anything. Finally, preserving the private sector's central role would stop program costs (and tax rates) from spiraling.

"Industry ought to take care of its own [welfare and employment] difficulties and problems," said one of Folsom's allies, Gerard Swope of General Electric, in testimony before a congressional committee in 1931.

> The moment government begins to help there is no economic restraint. You can vote the money. We would be glad to have the money, as anyone would; but the moment the General Electric Company or any industrial organization . . . provides for these various factors it is reflected in costs . . . and selling prices reflect costs; and therefore the people who use the product will ultimately pay for that [welfare] service; whereas, of course, if you vote the money by government assistance your general public will pay for it through taxation, which is very general and very indefinite.

The stature and thinking of Folsom, Swope, and other business leaders helped give New Dealers comfort (rightly, as it turned out) that business would come to live with government's modest new role in providing a social safety net. Folsom remained at the center of these debates for decades, eventually serving as deputy secretary of the Treasury and then secretary of health, education, and welfare under President Dwight Eisenhower in the 1950s. Folsom's lasting contribution was to implant a unique and pervasive business role into the genetic code of America's efforts to secure people against life's major risks. "In the end, what's notable about the New Deal is two things," says Jacob Hacker, the author of *The Divided Welfare State*. "One is that it was a huge breakthrough. The other is that it was also quite limited."

A MORTAL STRUGGLE

If the crisis of the Depression led to the birth of the modest American welfare state, the immediate postwar period saw the balance between public and private sector roles settled for half a century. The war years had witnessed unprecedented government involvement in the economy, and, as the servicemen came home, the question was what "the new normal" would look like. Europe was plainly growing comfortable with greater state control of private enterprise; Britain was working to implement a robust welfare state; and communism loomed as a viable alternative to many reformers abroad, not to mention its being a worrisome (if exaggerated) threat to a contingent in America.

It was in this pregnant moment that John L. Lewis, the towering, dictatorial leader of the United Mine Workers, took the bituminous coal workers out on strike in April 1946. Lewis, a poor, self-taught miner from Iowa who peppered his speeches with allusions to Shakespeare and had once punched a rival labor chief in the face, was considered an idiosyncratic opportunist by many of his union brethren. Yet there was no question that he had raised miners' living standards enormously. A Republican for most of his life who supported the New Deal before breaking with Franklin Roosevelt in 1940, Lewis had marched his followers out of the American Federation of Labor to form a rival labor group, the Congress of Industrial Organizations, in the mid-1930s, after the AFL balked at organizing unskilled mass production workers. Lewis repeatedly violated a pledge not to strike during wartime, most egregiously in 1943, when half a million miners walked off the job, crippling war production and angering the public. In an era when coal was the lifeblood of the economy, Lewis's ability to halt work at the mines made him one of the country's most powerful men.

When it came to benefits, Lewis had inherited the view of his old rival Samuel Gompers that the union should be in charge, not the state. So in the first postwar bargaining round, Lewis demanded that the coal companies finance a new health and welfare plan for miners that the union would run. The operators refused. Lewis took the miners out. After six weeks, a furious President Harry

Truman seized the mines and dispatched his secretary of the interior to work out a deal. The result was a groundbreaking agreement. The mine owners would pay for a new, independent medical and hospital plan as well as a retirement fund. The union would control the fund by naming two of the plan's three trustees. The operators would fund the plan via a royalty assessed on the amount of coal extracted by union workers. It was an industry-wide deal that appeared to give labor a dominant role in assuring workers' security. It took the employers' money but otherwise cut the employers out.

Corporate America, to put it mildly, freaked out. If the miners' model got traction, executives thought, it would be as bad as a full-fledged welfare state. But the threat also got business thinking. The spirit of capitalist introspection was exemplified by a widely debated manifesto in the pages of *Fortune,* written by Russell Davenport, a onetime managing editor of the magazine who had helped run Wendell Willkie's 1940 presidential campaign. Under the title "The Greatest Opportunity on Earth: There Is an Alternative to the 'Welfare State' and American Business Can Provide It," Davenport wrote in October 1949 that at that point in the nation's industrial evolution, workers' craving for economic security was legitimate. Yet socialism was the inevitable way this goal would be realized, he argued, unless business regained the initiative. "The business community has in the past committed the error of permitting government to assume the role of sole protector of the employee," Davenport wrote.

> If, for example, when the bottom dropped out of things in 1932, businessmen had taken the lead by insisting that government help *them* to implement the economic rights of their employees, the whole tenor of American history during the last two decades would have been different. Instead, business allowed Mr. Roosevelt to step into that heroic role. And Mr. Roosevelt and his heirs and

assigns have been shrewd enough to capitalize on it ever since. . . .
It is now time for the business community to show that corporate
action . . . can achieve the same result.

If business regained the upper hand by offering decent wages,
health care, and pensions, Davenport urged, it "would at a single
stroke cut through the socialist threat" and let business win what
he dubbed "a mortal struggle." And mortal it seemed. In Decem-
ber 1949, as the Congress of American Industry, a group of executives from the nation's largest firms, convened in New York,
Business Week reported the assembled executives' consensus that
"British socialism seems a closer threat than Russian communism."

The answer, business came to think, was to "double down" on
earlier, more modest forms of welfare capitalism. The rightward
lurch of postwar politics helped set the stage. In 1946, thanks to
inflation, war weariness, and rising fears of communism, the
Republican Party, campaigning on the slogan "Had Enough?," had
taken control of Congress for the first time since 1930. The Taft-
Hartley Act, passed over Truman's veto in the spring of 1947, cut
back on labor rights, partly in reaction to the mineworkers' coup.
Then Truman lost his battle for national health care in 1948 at the
hands of the American Medical Association. Just as business was
mulling creative ways to step up, in other words, Truman was
happy to see the impetus for economic security channeled into less
politicized channels such as collective bargaining.

WALTER'S DILEMMA

It was against this backdrop that Walter Reuther, the charismatic
leader of the United Auto Workers, made a fateful choice. Born in
West Virginia, Reuther had moved to the boomtown of Detroit to
work as a tool-and-die man for Ford, where he'd been fired in 1932
for socialist political activity. He came to prominence a few years

later when he led auto workers in bloody battles for union recognition at Ford and General Motors. Reuther survived two assassination attempts, the second of which left his right arm permanently damaged. But he was a visionary as well as a street fighter. "We aren't here for another nickel in the pay envelope," went Reuther's famous refrain. "We're here because the UAW is the vanguard of America!" Reuther saw collective bargaining as a way of pushing America's entire political economy toward social democratic ideals. Immensely popular, Reuther was also looked to by many liberals for creative leadership, and he delivered. A prime example was the major strike he led against GM in 1945, where he not only sought a 30 percent pay hike, but also made the unprecedented demand that the automaker open its books to show the public it could raise wages without raising prices.

As Reuther plotted his postwar strategy after winning the UAW presidency in 1946, he was at first skeptical of Lewis's breakthrough with the mine owners. A staunch Roosevelt man, Reuther had butted heads with Lewis during the war; if Lewis was for private, employer-financed benefits, the UAW chief reckoned, it had to be a reactionary idea. But when Republican control made further social legislation in Congress look unlikely, Reuther thought again. "At that point Reuther says, 'Okay, we tried hard to get national health insurance and better Social Security, and it didn't work,'" says Nelson Lichtenstein, the author of *The Most Dangerous Man in Detroit*, a biography of Reuther. "'So let's make these companies pay.'" The result, under Reuther's leadership, would be the negotiation of America's employer-centered welfare state.

To be sure, "the Treaty of Detroit," as the UAW-GM contract of 1950 was dubbed, was a milestone. The five-year contract delivered a 20 percent increase in living standards, pensions of $125 a month (a figure that meant something at the time), and new benefits for hospital and medical care. It was hailed by the national press as a turning point in industrial relations; some touted Reuther for president. But, as Reuther knew, for all that it achieved, the benefits portion of the deal represented a retreat from the UAW's vision, which was to transfer real resources from the company to union hands to secure the workers' welfare, as Lewis had done. But to the automakers (and the rest of American business), Lewis's model was a nonstarter. They would extend new benefits—Reuther found he was basically pushing on an open door here—but they would provide them only under management's strict control.

This helps explain why Reuther was conflicted by his victories. A committed social democrat, Reuther wanted the United States to imitate the more robust welfare states that Europe and Britain were building. He saw, or at least rationalized, his creation of business-centered health and pension programs as an interim step. If corporations became saddled with soaring benefit costs, he reasoned, they would join "shoulder to shoulder" with labor to demand that the federal government relieve them of this burden. "When you begin to put some pressure on their pocketbook nerve," Reuther said of corporate America, "they jump through hoops."

Reuther had played the political hand he was dealt. His aggressive leadership established the pattern for the postwar era, in which rising health and pension benefits from well-heeled employers allowed millions of workers without college degrees to live the middle-class American dream. But Reuther's bet that corporations would eventually see the light and fight for a bigger government role in providing benefits was a major miscalculation. Health and pension costs weren't nearly as high as they are today, and the financial pain Reuther thought these benefits would inflict never emerged. Instead, the unrivaled position of the U.S. economy after World War II, and the near-monopoly status this conferred on major U.S. firms, meant that the cost of corporately funded social welfare could (again) be passed on relatively easily via prices. Business's devotion to limited government in the face of creeping socialism abroad remained profound. Meanwhile, the victories of

Reuther and other union leaders at the bargaining table—which benefited only a portion of the nation's workforce—drained away the political energy that would have been needed to fuel a broader movement for change. Lewis, for his part, explicitly gave up support for national health care after the mine workers got their welfare deal. While Reuther never surrendered such goals, he found it hard to mobilize the beneficiaries of the private welfare state he had helped erect on behalf of similar gains for others. Reuther recognized soon enough that this had happened. "It is a very fundamental question of social policy," he told a congressional committee in 1957. "What is the relative emphasis that we ought to place upon . . . the public versus the private. We are in favor of a major emphasis upon the public sector, because that is the only instrument through which we can get universal coverage.

"But," Reuther added wistfully, "you cannot unscramble the omelet."

WHAT ARE THEY THINKING?

There would be little interest in unscrambling it for fifty years. In retrospect, the shortcomings of the employer-based benefit system were masked by fortuitous circumstances. Yes, the system left out people who weren't working, or who weren't married to a worker, or who worked at smaller firms that didn't offer coverage or subsidize it generously the way the big firms did. And yes, minorities and women tended to be underrepresented at the companies that offered decent health care and pensions. But during the first few decades after World War II, the typical home's economics were built around a breadwinning male who spent his career at a single firm. American business was on top of the world. Spending on health as a percentage of GDP was only 5 percent in 1960 and 7 percent in 1970. And when obvious gaps in the employer-based system grew intolerable—for example, as concerns rose that the

elderly, who had left employment, were essentially uninsurable—
the political system eventually responded, with the enactment of
such programs as Medicare.

But now, of course, we're in a vastly different world than the
one Marion Folsom and Walter Reuther helped make, back when
halting the slippery slope to socialism was business's tacit aim for
U.S. policy. Since the fall of the Berlin Wall and the end of the Cold
War, socialism has been discredited as an economic system. The
pendulum has now swung toward markets. Global competition
has ended the unique dominance of American firms, and with it
the pricing freedom that effectively subsidized benefits and made
the employer-based system viable. Workers now change jobs many
times in the course of a career; tens of millions are permanent
"free agents," unattached to traditional jobs that bring benefits.
"Job lock"—the phenomenon through which people stay in jobs
they'd rather leave because they can't afford to lose their health
coverage—has entered the lexicon, hurting the economy's dyna-
mism and dampening entrepreneurship.

Health costs have become staggering. America spends 16 percent of GDP on health care, with that number expected to rise to
20 percent by 2015, while other advanced nations average 11 percent. Yet those nations cover everyone, while America leaves nearly
50 million people uninsured; and the United States does not boast
better public health outcomes. In aggregate, American employers
now spend roughly $600 billion on health care and $200 billion on
pensions, costs that no other advanced nation imposes on its companies. It's crazy but true: Starbucks spends more on health care
than on coffee; General Motors spends more on health care than
on steel. Yet while these firms can tell you everything about the coffee and steel they buy, companies remain shockingly ignorant of
what they're getting for these trillions they spend on employee
health.

The situation with retirement is equally discouraging. Defined benefit pensions, a staple of the world Reuther helped shape, now cover just 15 percent of the workforce, down from 40 percent in the mid-1970s. Those firms that still do offer retirement benefits have shifted to defined contribution plans in droves. (In a defined benefit plan, the retiree receives a guaranteed pension payment each month, financed by the company; in a defined contribution plan—such as a 401(k)—the employer makes a fixed contribution to a retirement fund to which the employee may add his own money, with the employee eventually making withdrawals based on the account's investment performance over the intervening years.) Seventy-five million full-time workers do not have a savings or retirement plan beyond Social Security. Toss in Social Security's looming woes, and no wonder experts say that tens of millions of workers won't be able to maintain their pre-retirement standard of living after they stop working.

It's not a pretty picture. More employers drop traditional health and pension coverage every year, and more voters tell pollsters they feel insecure. This anxiety has become a potent political force.

Yet despite these radically changed circumstances, and the threats that health and pension costs pose to business's bottom line and public image, corporate America remains caught in a time warp in its attitude toward government. Health care offers the most vexing illustration. Business resolutely resists the idea of government assuring a basic minimum coverage (along the lines of Social Security providing a universal basic retirement benefit) that might supplant its own current funding and administrative role. Inexplicably, business's message to Uncle Sam seems to be, "Whatever you do, don't get me off the hook for this mess." When you ask business leaders why this is the case—why Americans in the twenty-first century should still look to their employers, not their country, for such support—you bump up against uncharacteristically muddled thinking or non sequiturs, sure signs that something beyond reason is at work. "If I've got a good health care program that you can go home and tell Muriel about, I've got a better chance of recruiting you than the guy down the street who doesn't have one," says Tom Donahue, the president of the U.S. Chamber of Commerce, by way of explanation. But if government assured a basic benefit, surely companies could still lure talent with supplemental offerings. "We'll end up paying for it anyway, and we won't have control over the costs this time," says John Castellani, the president of the Business Roundtable. But our employer-based system already delivers the costliest health care on the planet. That hardly makes a case that it's the answer. Business won't pay, or won't pay as much as it does today, if the powerful business lobby makes *permanently lowering business's contribution to health costs* its reform aim, rather than mindlessly fighting off government altogether. Steve Burd, Safeway's CEO, says that if government picked up the tab we'd lose the innovation and efficiency that companies like his bring to bear. But that's not clear either. The Veterans Administration health care system, for example, has been hailed as the leader in using technology and evidence-based medicine to improve health while lowering costs. And most ambitious health reform proposals ask government to take to scale the preventive care ideas that Safeway and others have helped pilot. Besides, on Burd's logic, Safeway ought to be running its own schools for employees, too, and raising its own army to protect them. That can't be right. So what's really going on in the corporate mind?

History and common sense suggest only one answer: corporate America's reflexive antigovernment ideology now stands in the way of its self-interest. This reflex is hardly new, but to the extent that it now stops America from adapting successfully to the global economy, this mind-set has become an economic threat in itself. Business originally resisted many government actions that have become widely supported fixtures of American life: child labor laws, the Federal Reserve, the Securities and Exchange Commission, Social Security, the Marshall Plan, national parks, federal aid to education,

Medicare. The list is endless, and embarrassing. "Often it fought them with such gruesome predictions of awful consequences to our private enterprise system," wrote Theodore Levitt of the Harvard Business School in 1968, "that one wonders how the foretellers of such doom can now face themselves in the mirror each morning and still believe themselves competent to make important decisions on major matters in their own companies."

None of this means business needs to love government, or overlook its idiocies and inefficiencies. (I've worked at senior levels in both sectors, and while government has problems, business ain't perfect either, as businesspeople well know.) It just means realizing, as executives in every other advanced nation do, that government plays a legitimate, indispensable role in assuring the provision of certain public goods. This kind of common sense is virtually taboo in American business today. One prominent Republican billionaire I know—who is appalled by our health care woes and who is outspoken on just about every other subject—refuses to go on record with his private view that government should provide a basic benefit via some kind of single payer plan and let folks who want more coverage add private plans on top. The gang at the club just wouldn't understand. Carl Camden, the CEO of Kelly Services, whose "free agent" work force has sensitized him to the inanity of the American way of health, says that for too many CEOs, "blind allegiance to free market principles has obscured the fact that our system isn't working and that health care can't be a free market anyway."

Andrew Stern, the president of the Service Employees International Union, says that for twenty years employers told him to "get into the twentieth century." Those old-style union ideas of the 1930s, '40s, and '50s just didn't make sense anymore, he was lectured. These CEOs were right, Stern acknowledges; labor had to change. "Now I say to them, 'Get into the *twenty-first* century,'" he says. "'Employer-based healthcare is dead, employer-based pensions

are dead, and you guys are relics of another era.' The people who
were telling us we were dinosaurs are actually the dinosaurs of
today."

THE OPENING OF THE CAPITALIST MIND

Once the capitalist mind opens there will be no shortage of fixes.
Take health care. The long-standing worry of American business—
that a greater government role invariably means a slide to a
Canadian-style single payer system—has been leapfrogged by the
call for "market-based universal coverage" issued in 2007 by the
Committee for Economic Development. The CED is a business-led
think tank founded in 1942 by a group of prominent executives,
including Marion Folsom. Its report doesn't mince words: "The
nation needs a new system to replace employer-provided health
insurance." The CED would offer people access to private group
coverage via regional insurance exchanges, and would subsidize
lower-income folks who need help. Over time they'd like government to pay for a basic plan for everyone, and fund it via a consumption or value-added tax. The system would include new
incentives for health delivery systems to compete on value. Says
the CED's president, Charles Kolb: "Business needs to wake up and
rethink this if we're going to compete in a global economy and do
right by ordinary Americans."

I asked John Castellani, the president of the Business Roundtable, why another business group was coming down differently
from his organization, which wants to keep employers at the center of things. Castellani thought a moment, then said maybe it's
because CED is comprised mainly of retired CEOs, whereas the
Roundtable's CEOs are still active. I'm not sure what that means.
Why would active CEOs want to have business continue to bear
more of the health care burden? It doesn't make sense. And maybe
that's the point: the persistence of business's determination to

remain at the heart of America's welfare system doesn't make sense. I suspect the real difference between the Business Round-table and the CED is that active CEOs are under the sway of their naysaying human resources departments, whose benefits empires are threatened by fundamental change. The missing ingredient in every health care reform plan is a generous buyout package for human resources chiefs at the Fortune 500, whom politicians in both parties privately tell me are part of the problem.

It's time to declare victory and move on. America vanquished communism and socialism after an epic struggle, and the employer-based benefit system deserves its share of the credit for the triumph. But that century-old strategic choice set in motion political patterns and habits of mind that have calcified to the point where we can't do what global competitiveness and social justice now require. The only force that can break this logjam is business, and business can only do it by looking at the facts and *changing its mind*. We won't become socialist. We'll still need to address costs. Firms that want to can still serve as facilitators (if not primary funders) of coverage for their employees. And none of this means business is "walking away from the problem"; indeed, business will need, more than ever, to be a constituency for the changes that are necessary. All this is doable. But one tumbler first has to click into place. Sooner or later, business has to realize that when it comes to its pervasive role in America's welfare state, it's okay, and sensible, to let go.

4

TAXES HURT THE ECONOMY (AND THEY'RE ALWAYS TOO HIGH)

*In which it becomes apparent that taxes are
going up in the next decade no matter who is in power,
and that the economy will be just fine*

In 1883, Adolf Wagner, a combative forty-eight-year-old German economist, was puzzling over the way modern societies evolved. It had been two years since Otto von Bismarck had persuaded the emperor William I to send an extraordinary message to parliament that by decade's end would lead to the creation of the first modern system of social security. "The healing of social wrongs must be sought . . . by positively advancing the well-being of the workers," William wrote, with uncharacteristic empathy. "Those who are disabled from work by age and invalidity have a well-grounded claim to care from the state." Bismarck, as canny and brutal a statesman as existed in the nineteenth century, was hardly a softheaded liberal, but he came under vicious attack from the right for promoting such left-wing ideas. "Call it socialism or anything you like," Bismarck sputtered at his critics, who didn't grasp his plan to blunt the more radical agenda of Karl Marx and Friedrich Engels. "It is all the same to me."

The whole controversy got Wagner thinking. As people grew more affluent, he reasoned, they'd want more of what only government could provide—a strong military, public order, good schools, and assorted welfare benefits, services that private citizens would have trouble arranging for on their own. As a result of these desires, Wagner predicted, the development of an industrial economy would be accompanied by an increased share of public expenditure in gross national product. This simple insight, known as Wagner's Law to economists today, explains much that we've observed in the century or so since. Industrial nations have much higher taxes, measured as a percentage of their economy, than do poorer nations, and similarly they have higher spending on health care, schools, pensions, police, and so forth. As it turns out, no one sent the memo about Wagner's Law to the modern Republican Party. Which is roughly how a Reagan foot soldier named Bruce Bartlett came to be excommunicated from the conservative movement in 2003.

In the fall of that year, Bartlett was stumped. A former economic aide in the Reagan White House and a Treasury official under George H. W. Bush, Bartlett was a libertarian, small-government think tank scholar who had watched with amusement as the debate raged over adding a prescription drug benefit to Medicare. He presumed that President George W. Bush's support for the bill was insincere; the sausage the Republican Congress was cooking up would be such an unprecedented budget-buster, costing trillions in the decades ahead, that Bush had to be playing his part in a classic Washington minuet. Everyone knew the drill: the Senate and House would pass different versions of the measure that couldn't possibly be reconciled; the drug bill would thus die an unavoidable but "regretted" death; all sides would claim credit for having supported fresh aid for America's seniors; they'd return to fight the good fight another day. This had to be what was going on, Bartlett reckoned, because the White House was sending signals that it would sign any bill that passed. No president could be that fiscally reckless, Bartlett knew.

But President Bush, who wanted to be reelected in 2004, saw things differently. Bush knew in his political gut that Adolf Wagner was right, and that the moment had come to give struggling seniors the public help they sought for costly medicines. "I suddenly realized, this wasn't a game at all," Bartlett recalls. "They wanted to get this thing passed and they didn't care what was in it. It was like a cold slap in the face." Like many conservatives, Bartlett was outraged when the president signed the pricey new benefit into law. Then, like any good policy wonk, he sat down to think through what it all meant.

The government already faced about $40 trillion in unfunded liabilities for programs such as Social Security and Medicare. Bush and the Republican Party had just put their imprimatur on trillions more. Bartlett's conclusion was merely mathematical. "We cannot avoid a massive tax increase sometime in the near future," he recalls realizing. For a Republican to think such a thought was bad enough. Then Bartlett committed his real crime. He began laying out this thinking in public, first in his syndicated column and then in magazine articles. Bartlett argued that it was now clear beyond disputing that the Republican Party, despite its rhetoric, would never slow spending growth: after all, it had just enacted the biggest new health care entitlement since the 1960s, even as it balked at cutting a few billion dollars from the next trillion in planned Medicaid spending for the poor. Since tax increases would therefore be necessary before long to avoid untenable and debilitating deficits, the country needed to think about how to raise new revenue in ways that would be least distorting for the economy. To Bartlett, that meant it was time for an American version of the national sales tax favored by many European governments: a value added tax, or VAT.

Conservative Washington went berserk. Bartlett was summoned to a meeting at the Heritage Foundation, where several right-wing analysts castigated him for his heresy. Why are you endorsing tax increases, they demanded to know. To Bartlett the accusation was surreal. I'm not *endorsing* tax increases, he replied; I'm forecasting them. You know the facts as well as I do. "They simply refused to accept those realities," Bartlett recalls. "They refused to confront the numbers as they exist." Before long, Bartlett became persona non grata on the right, a man without a party. His banishment stood as a warning to others not to stray from the party line on taxes, no matter how detached from reality the orthodoxy became.

"I'm not in favor of higher taxes," Bartlett told me several years later, still smarting. "I'd be all in favor of slashing government so that it was not necessary. But I'm not stupid. I can see that we're not going to do that. We're not going to cut tens of trillions of dollars out of future spending from large constituencies of voters who are dependent upon these programs. It just isn't going to happen. And anybody who thinks it is, is living in a dream world."

DESTINY AND DENIAL

Some Dead Ideas, like the idea that "Your Company Should Take Care of You," represent a response to broad historical forces that alter our institutions and over time become entrenched in popular consciousness as "the way things work." But others, like the notion that "Taxes Hurt the Economy and They're Always Too High," have different origins. This idea, which in various forms has recurred throughout human history, is born in the self-interest of the small number of people who typically control most of the resources in a society, because, given the choice, they would prefer to avoid sharing those resources with others. Though Wagner's Law suggests that from history's viewpoint, society's "haves" may be fighting a losing battle (and, in addition, that the broad middle will happily tax itself for services it comes to want), that doesn't mean the wealthy can't win important skirmishes along the way. Indeed, the fact that taxes remain relatively low in America (compared to other advanced nations), when the top 5 percent of the population control half or more of the nation's wealth but wield only 5 percent of its votes, suggests how powerful the antitax idea has been. Partly that's because the "haves" hire skilled propagandists to persuade the public that taxes of any kind are destructive. Partly it's because at some level, taxes do distort incentives and hurt the economy—as was the case with the 70 percent marginal income tax rates that applied before Ronald Reagan took office in 1981. For thirty years in the United States, the conservative movement, aided by liberal excess and ineptitude, has successfully shaped political debate along these lines. But now, as a conservative like Bruce Bartlett realized when he penciled it out, the antitax idea is doomed. What's more, as we'll see, if we do things right, the economy will be as strong as ever (and in many ways stronger) as taxes rise in the years ahead.

To see why the modern antitax idea is dead, we must first understand that taxes are going up *no matter who is in power.* Don't take my word for it. Listen to some of today's preeminent Republican budget analysts. Like every Republican who aspires to serve in a public role, they've been schooled by the party's antitax police to avoid saying things too definitively, or to leave themselves an "if we only got tough on spending" escape hatch, a ploy we've seen is a charade thanks to Republicans' repeated refusal to trim spending when they actually controlled every corner of Washington. So there's no mistaking what these folks are saying.

"If you do nothing on the spending side, you're going to raise taxes whether you're a Republican, a Democrat, or a Martian," says Douglas Holtz-Eakin, the Republican-appointed director of the Congressional Budget Office from 2003 to 2005, who served as the top economic adviser to John McCain's presidential campaign. "It's arithmetic." Federal revenue today is 18.8 percent of GDP and federal spending is 20 percent. Holtz-Eakin observes that "the pressures are there" to lift spending and taxes to 23 or 24 percent of GDP by around 2020, and to as much as 27 percent if health costs remain out of control. Note that in the context of a $14 trillion economy, he's predicting (at the low end) a $550 billion to $700 billion tax increase per year, in today's dollars.

David Walker is a Republican who served as comptroller general of the United States from 1998 to 2008, when he left to run the Peter G. Peterson Foundation. As head of the Government Accountability Office, he was part of a national "Fiscal Wake-Up Tour" in recent years that called attention to our long-run budget woes, a campaign he is expanding in his new role. Walker told me when we spoke in his government office that taxes would grow to 20 to 25 percent of GDP within twenty years, depending on how "radical" we get about spending cuts. Since, as we've seen, serious spending cuts are unlikely, it's fair to interpret Walker's projection as being closer to 25 percent of GDP than to 20 percent.

Over lunch one day during the recent presidential campaign, I spoke with another highly respected economic analyst in John McCain's circle. (The ground rules for our conversation were that I could not attribute these comments to this person, because a "straight talker" like McCain could not be seen to be advised by someone who actually talked straight on taxes!)

Are taxes going up? I asked.

"Yeah," the McCain adviser said. "I think it is inevitable."

"If you were a betting man at this point, are taxes going to be higher as a share of GDP in 2020?"

"Definitely."

"How much higher?"

"I don't know."

"Ballpark?"

"Twenty-two [percent of GDP]," this person replied. "But 2020 is still a little bit at the front end of the boomers. You can figure twenty-four, twenty-five by 2030."

"Let's say we're at twenty-two in 2020, up from eighteenish today," I said. "Is that some disaster for the economy? Will it really make a big difference?"

"Probably not," the adviser said. "Depends on how you do it, of course."

So: the consensus of three professional Republican budgeteers is that taxes will rise by between 4 percent and 7 percent of GDP over the next ten to twenty years, translating (in today's dollars) into $550 billion to $1 trillion more in new annual taxes. You heard it here first: the Republicans have a secret plan to raise taxes. So do the Democrats, of course, and well beyond the rollback of the Bush tax cuts for the top they felt safe discussing during the 2008 presidential campaign.

The gap between our destiny and our denial on taxes is one of the most consequential chasms in American public life. Not to mention curious. If higher taxes are inevitable (and, as we'll see, the economy will do just fine in spite of them), how did we get to the point where the prevailing idea in the American mind is the opposite—that taxes hurt the economy and they're always too high?

TAX WARS: THE BRIEF HISTORY

Tax debates may be the purest example history offers of the truth of Ambrose Bierce's wonderful line in *The Devil's Dictionary*, where he defines politics as "a strife of interests masquerading as a contest of principles; the conduct of public affairs for private advantage." An impossibly brief (and therefore highly selective) review of Everything You Need to Know About U.S. Tax History yields three important lessons. First, the arguments over taxes never change. Second, the economy has grown larger and more productive even as government spending and taxes have risen. Third, it generally takes a war or other national crisis to bring significant changes in the way we tax ourselves.

Let's plunge in. More than two thousand years ago, Aristotle noted that in a democracy the masses might use their numbers and political clout to gang up on the rich and redistribute their wealth, but for most of history this hasn't happened. If anything, its been plunder from above. The United States has been no exception, though our evolving tax regime has been misleadingly described. Modern conservatives like to say that a country born in a tax revolt comes by its tax loathing naturally, but that's a gross misreading of the Boston Tea Party and the founders' ideas. The colonies resented taxation *without representation,* not taxes generally; Americans matter-of-factly raised revenue for roads, schools, and other common purposes. Early antitax sentiment was less about innate American revulsion than about specific interests who feared the prospect of federal authority. The leading examples, as the historian Robin Einhorn of the University of California, Berkeley, has shown, were large southern slaveholders, who wouldn't sanction any federal power that might permit the national government to tax slavery out of existence. Einhorn argues that the slaveholding class's shrewd campaign against big government in America's early decades, whose propaganda featured threats to iconic yeoman farmers at the hands of the overbearing feds, was the first case of financial elites cynically (and successfully) posing as tribunes of the common man to preserve their own prerogatives.

Partly as a result, federal taxes from Alexander Hamilton's days as secretary of the Treasury all the way up to World War I were basically regressive—meaning that the lower and middle classes shouldered a larger proportionate burden than did those at the top. Throughout the nineteenth century the federal government's revenue came primarily from tariffs on imported goods, which raised prices across the board and were thus effectively paid by ordinary citizens. The federal government also imposed excise taxes on goods like alcohol and cigarettes. Among other things, this so upset small farmer-distillers that it sparked the Whiskey Rebellion in 1794, during which President George Washington personally led twelve thousand troops into western Pennsylvania to put down the insurrection and assert the authority of the young national government.

To be sure, the tariff system designed by Hamilton proved effective. As we've seen, the protection it offered helped nascent American industries develop. It enabled the United States to pay off the national debt (incurred during wars) by 1835. It generated enough revenue thereafter to support internal improvements like canals, and to let Uncle Sam offer federal lands on generous terms to low and middle income settlers, boosting western growth and providing opportunity for millions. In the 1850s, 92 percent of federal revenue came from customs duties imposed on imports.

Still, despite these successes, trouble was brewing over how the tax burden was borne, sentiment that spilled into politics during the decades-long battle over whether America should have an income tax. Steven Weisman, the author of *The Great Tax Wars* (a superb chronicle that informs much of the account below), argues that these historic debates involved a showdown between two values: justice and virtue. Justice meant seeing the income tax as a kind of leveler, not necessarily redistributing wealth (it wasn't seen this way early on) but softening the edges of inequality as unprecedented industrial fortunes emerged. By contrast, opponents of the income tax spoke of virtue—of the hard work, thrift, ingenuity, and risk taking that formed the foundation of capitalism. In this view, taxing people at higher rates if they earned more was tantamount to punishing virtue, and distorted the incentives on which prosperity rested. Sound familiar?

The first great clash came during the Civil War, when the federal government needed enormous new sums to wage war and secure massive loans. There were practical limits to how much money tariffs could raise, and fairness concerns as well. It was uncomfortable enough in a democracy that wealthy men could pay to avoid service in the Union army. But would the rich, including the many manufacturers making a fortune from the war effort, be permitted to contribute little to its colossal cost? Wartime inflation pinched the man in the street while the makers of guns, medicines, and uniforms raked in millions. An article in *Harper's* magazine entitled "The Fortunes of War" catalogued the speculators and federal contractors who were getting rich on the general misery, adding that the cost of a dinner at Delmonico's in New York could "support a soldier and his family for a good portion of a year." The brewing resentment would contribute to an explosion in 1863, when four days of draft riots in New York led to the deaths of a thousand people. Six thousand federal troops had to be called in to restore order.

An income tax—a new idea—emerged as part of the answer to the inequity. But policy makers knew they were crossing into uncharted territory. Representative Justin Morrill of Vermont, of the House Ways and Means Committee, quoted John Milton's *Paradise Lost,* comparing the American taxpayer to Adam and Eve, driven by necessity "from our untaxed garden." But Morrill also spoke of fairness. "Ought not men . . . with large incomes, to pay more in proportion to what they have than those with limited means, who live by the work of their own hands or that of their families?" Thaddeus Stevens, the abolitionist chairman of the committee, wanted an income tax with graduated rates scaled to "the ability to pay." "It would be manifestly unjust," he said, "to allow the large money operators and wealthy merchants . . . to escape from their fair proportion of the burden." The *Chicago Tribune* was more direct: "The rich should pay more than the poor." The law finally enacted had two rates: 3 percent on income above $600, and 5 percent on income above $10,000. (Remember, this was 1862.) The Confederacy, unwilling to raise taxes, was in financial turmoil;

it printed money to pay bills, creating disastrous inflation. "For God's sake, tax us!" cried the editor of the *Richmond Enquirer.*

Yet efforts to make the federal income tax a little more progressive two years later met with resistance even from supporters of the previous measure. It was "vicious" and "unjust" to enact a "punishment of the rich man because he is rich," Thaddeus Stevens now said, adding that unequal tax rates were "no less than a confiscation of property." Rich men would leave the country rather than pay the tax, foes added. Not everyone agreed. "Go to the Astors and Stewarts and other rich men of the country and ask them if in the midst of a war [the income tax] is unreasonable," countered one lawmaker during the House debate. "I could not advocate anything else in justice to the middle classes of the country." Some made the audacious argument that higher rates on the rich diminished the standing of poor men, as if being left out of the income tax would hurt their feelings. "It is seizing property of men for the crime of having too much!" one senator said. Another senator, while acknowledging that richer folks could afford to pay, nonetheless argued that "an odious and ungenerous discrimination against the rich" could wreck American prosperity.

UPS AND DOWNS

Once the wartime emergency passed, wealthy forces mobilized, and the income tax (along with a wartime inheritance tax) was repealed within seven years. At its peak in 1867 the income tax raised 24 percent of federal revenue. Most historians say that only about 1 percent of Americans were ever subject to the tax. Repeal meant that the huge federal debt left over from the Civil War, held mostly by well-to-do Americans, had to be serviced by tariff revenues whose burden was felt almost entirely by average citizens.

Yet even as debate over repeal of the income tax raged between 1870 and 1872, the logic for its resurrection was being laid. Senator

John Sherman of Ohio, later of antitrust law fame, said the burden imposed by tariffs and excise taxes was simply wrong. "We tax the tea, the coffee, the sugar, and the spices the poor man uses," he said in 1870. "We tax every little thing that is imported from abroad, together with the whisky that makes him drunk and the beer that cheers him and the tobacco that consoles him. Everything that he consumes we call a luxury and tax it; yet we are afraid to touch the income of Mr. Astor. Is there any justice in that?"

The battle lay dormant for a generation. Then the Panic of 1893, and the lengthy depression that followed, sparked fresh outrage over the deprivation of ordinary people compared to the grandeur enjoyed by the wealthy few. Unemployment reached 20 percent. Industrial unrest grew. Farmers reeled from price declines. And stunning revelations appeared in the press about how the rich were shirking their share. An article in *Forum*, a leading magazine, entitled "The Owners of the United States," profiled the handful of families that now owned a greater share of the national wealth than did Britain's upper crust: the Vanderbilts, Huntingtons, Morgans, Drexels, and their ilk. While federal taxation had increased sixfold since 1860, the article explained, the tab had been picked up primarily by lower income Americans. The magnitude of the inequity was captured by a stunning fact: as one expert testified to Congress, an income tax of just 2.5 percent would allow for a 25 percent reduction in tariffs, hugely aiding middle and lower earners. William Jennings Bryan took up the cause, crying on the House floor in 1894 that opponents of an income tax "weep more because 15 millions are to be collected from the incomes of the rich than they do at the collection of 300 millions upon the goods which the poor consume."

Foes of the tax said it would discriminate against the (wealthier) north; encourage fraud (because people would lie about their income); depress real estate; kill the stock market; and hurt business. They also said (again) that the rich would flee the country—to which Bryan replied famously "Whither will they fly?" citing income taxes that by then existed in countries across Europe. Senator David Bennet Hill insisted that the tax was an idea imported to America by "little squads of anarchists, communists and socialists." Yet many proponents urged it paradoxically as a conservative step that could help keep a lid on rising class anger and resentment. Representative Uriel Hall, a Missouri Democrat, called it "a measure to kill anarchy and keep down socialists." When the dust cleared, the measure that finally passed in 1894 would have affected only 2 percent of Americans, imposing a 2 percent tax on incomes over $4,000. Then the Supreme Court (for reasons too arcane to detain us here) ruled the measure unconstitutional. The *New York Tribune* said "the fury of ignorant class hatred has dashed itself in vain against the Constitution." The *New York World* called the court's decision "a triumph of selfishness."

THE HIGHER TAX CENTURY

To make a long story short, it took eighteen more years of debate before a constitutional amendment was enacted in 1913 that made the income tax legal. Democrats, suspicious of increasingly concentrated wealth and power, saw their campaign against the protective tariff and in favor of the income tax as two planks of the same general policy: the measures offered relief for ordinary Americans, and struck a blow against corrupt practices by business elites that effectively picked the little guy's pocket. Republicans, for their part, said taxation according to "ability to pay" would punish enterprise, savings, and investment; give rise to an intrusive army of tax bureaucrats; and pit rich against poor. Businesses thriving under protectionism also privately feared that the income tax would prove so attractive a revenue source that there would be pressure to end the system of tariffs altogether. In the debate over the constitutional amendment, the *Albany Evening Journal,* a Republican paper, said that the tax would "divide the population into two classes, the class which contributes to the support of the Government, and the class which does not contribute," a ludicrous argument given that the supposed deadbeats actually paid the bulk of federal taxes via customs duties and excise levies. (This rhetorical strategy was a forerunner of what we see on the *Wall Street Journal* editorial page today, which routinely claims that the rich pay the lion's share of federal revenue, ignoring the giant payroll tax paid mostly by middle and lower income citizens.) But as the historian W. Elliot Brownlee points out, when President Woodrow Wilson finally signed into law an income tax that could pass constitutional muster in 1913, virtually none of the tax's proponents thought it would become a major, permanent source of revenue in the federal system.

The two world wars changed all that. On the eve of World War I, tariffs and excise taxes brought in 90 percent of federal revenue. Then federal spending rose from $742 million in 1916 to almost $14 billion in 1918, with the income tax funding the rise. The federal budget for a single year had suddenly grown nearly equal to all the spending the federal government had done from 1791 to that time. Effective income tax rates on wealthier households jumped from 3 percent to 15 percent, with marginal rates for the wealthiest topping 60 percent.

But World War II witnessed the truly epochal shift. Before Social Security was enacted in the mid-1930s, it would have been impractical to administer a mass income tax; the federal government simply didn't have the information it would have needed on taxpayers and incomes, or a method like withholding with which to enlist employers in efficient revenue collection. Now it did. The war took the number of Americans paying income tax from 4 million in 1939 to 43 million in 1945; revenues rose from $2.2 billion to $35 billion. Needless to say, this represented an extraordinary change for the nation, and was accompanied by a massive public relations campaign. Irving Berlin wrote a patriotic song entitled "I Paid My Income Tax Today." The federal government commissioned a short film from Disney called *The New Spirit,* in which Donald Duck, stunned by his new income tax bill, has a headache and takes an aspirin before learning that he can handle it all. He travels to Washington and learns that the money is being used to build warships to defeat the Nazis. In the end, Donald is glad to pay his taxes. Similar messages were stitched into popular radio programs like *The George Burns Show.* By all accounts, the pitches were effective.

Federal receipts rose from 7 to 21 percent of GDP during the war, as spending surged from between 8 and 10 percent of GDP in the late 1930s to more than 43 percent of GDP by war's end. Far from hurting the economy, these increases powered the country out of depression. They also set the stage for the massive postwar boom, which took place with the federal government consuming permanently higher levels of revenue and spending (these settled in the mid to high teens as a percentage of GDP by the late 1940s and early 1950s). Just as important, both parties tacitly agreed to keep the new tax regime and levels, and to embrace the use of fiscal policy as a form of macroeconomic management. As we saw in chapter 1, the economy thrived, even though top marginal tax rates in the 1950s were as high as 87 percent, and stood at 70 percent after 1964.

BACKLASH

By now, the backlash against taxes and "big government" that emerged in the 1970s and 1980s is a familiar story. Growth slowed. Oil shocks and inflation, combined with a growing sense that liberals had been ineffectively throwing money at the poor, left an increasing number of voters weary and frustrated. The payroll taxes that funded Social Security and Medicare continued their stealthy rise; a system funded originally with payroll taxes of 2 percent of wages was (thanks to ever-rising benefits) on its way well past the 10 percent level that politicians worried would lead to taxpayer resistance. With pocketbooks pinched and wages stagnating, and with inflation pushing people into higher income tax brackets, resentment simmered. Then California's Proposition 13 showed in 1978 that taxes could spark a potent political brushfire. The Republican Party leaped to seize the issue.

The seminal change was in Republican thinking. Traditionally, the party had been fiscally conservative and made a virtue of balanced budgets. But the new Republican stars, like Jack Kemp and Ronald Reagan, saw the tax cut message as a tremendous political opportunity—never mind that Reagan had passed the biggest tax increases in state history while serving as governor of California. They also thought tax reductions could help jolt the anemic economy. But rhetoric aside, the politicians certainly didn't want to be bothered with the unpleasant work of cutting spending as well. Luckily for them, intellectual justification suddenly emerged for saying "Deficits be damned." Economists like Milton Friedman and editorialists like Jude Wanniski of the *Wall Street Journal* argued that "starve the beast" was a perfectly defensible way to limit the size of government. Cut taxes first, they counseled, and spending would eventually have to come into line. And if it didn't, well, that was no big deal either. It might even be salutary, since deficits would put new political restraints on the amount of spending that would otherwise occur. The economist Arthur Laffer sketched his notorious curve on a napkin to show that cutting taxes might actually increase government revenue. Though these assertions turned out to be bogus, they proved irresistible to Republican politicians, and the party's love affair with tax cuts began. Soon a well-funded infrastructure of conservative think tanks and institutes made sure that the new thinking on taxes permeated every corner of the capital.

The Republicans were particularly successful in the 1980s and early 1990s in demonizing the tiny fraction of the budget that went to welfare. They also deftly separated the idea of taxes in the American mind from the popular things (health care, pensions, schools) that tax revenues paid for. This schizophrenia was a stunning conservative achievement. As one angry senior citizen cried to a senator in the 1990s, "Don't let the government get its hands on my Medicare!"

By the turn of the century the debate had settled into well-worn grooves. Republicans were for more tax cuts no matter what: in bad times they were the road to recovery; in good times they were critical to keep a boom rolling. When I worked in the White House in the early 1990s, President Clinton told his advisers that the Republican tax message worked. He described how economically strapped voters reasoned, as follows: "We can't trust any of these damn politicians, but at least the Republicans will give me some of my money back." In an era of wage stagnation, this hard-bitten logic has proved a powerful lure. Even if most tax cuts went to the top, the average guy still got a few bucks. Republicans designed their plans to be sure this was the case. Democrats, meanwhile, knowing how powerful the issue was for families who felt squeezed, were afraid not to be "for" tax cuts, too. So they offered "targeted" tax cuts (for kids or for savings, for example) in the hope that this would still leave enough money in the till for programs they liked. And there the debate still stands—with both parties, for different reasons, unwilling to discuss the certain tax increases in America's future.

THE EVIDENCE, PLEASE

So what do we need to know about the impact of taxes on the economy—and, in particular, about the impact of higher aggregate taxes than we have today, since that's what's coming? Economists distinguish between micro effects and macro effects. Micro, which deals with the impact of taxes on how much people work and save, or how much research and development firms do, tends to get the lion's share of the profession's attention. The conclusions, shorn of the fancy math, aren't hard to understand. Incentives matter. If you lower the financial return on an activity, some people are going to be dissuaded from doing it. If unemployment benefits are too generous, people are less likely to work. If marginal tax rates are 90 percent, ditto. David Stockman, Ronald Reagan's budget director, said Reagan's own experience had seared into him the truth of this lesson. After World War II, Reagan told Stockman, when marginal rates hovered around 90 percent, he would stop making movies when he hit that bracket, and take it easy for the rest of the year. "You want to take seriously what the economic cost is of having high taxes," says Joel Slemrod, an economist at the University of Michigan and a coauthor of the book *Taxing Ourselves*. "The micro effects can be important in some situations, but they're overstated in general in the U.S. policy debate."

Yet while economists quarrel about the precise micro impact of taxes on various activities, the more interesting macro story gets no attention at all. The question here is: What is the effect of higher aggregate taxes and spending on the level and growth rate of national income? The fascinating truth is what Adolf Wagner predicted 125 years ago: wealthier nations tend to have higher taxes and spending. And America's taxes and spending can rise substantially from where they are today with little or no impact on the economy.

This can be seen from several angles. The first, which we've touched on indirectly in our march through America's tax wars, compares today with our past. In the last century or so, America's living standards, as measured by output per person, have increased sevenfold. Yet, as we've seen, taxes and spending as a share of GDP were very low in the nineteenth century, and now hover around 19 or 20 percent of GDP. The 1950s and 1960s, the period of our fastest growth in productivity, were also the era of our highest marginal

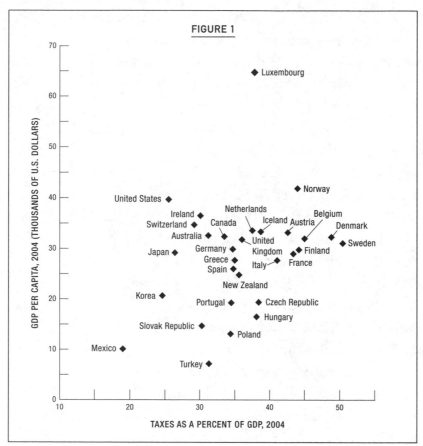

FIGURE 1

Y-axis: GDP PER CAPITA, 2004 (THOUSANDS OF U.S. DOLLARS)

X-axis: TAXES AS A PERCENT OF GDP, 2004

Source: Joel Slemrod, University of Michigan

tax rates. That obviously doesn't mean these tax rates caused the growth, but it suggests that other forces are much more important in driving the economy.

Then there are international comparisons. First, let's compare the level of taxes in the advanced nations with their incomes. Figure 1 does just that; on the left axis you see real income per person (or GDP per capita); on the right, taxes as a percentage of GDP. If higher taxes spelled the death knell for prosperity, we would expect to see the points clustering on a line that starts on the upper left and heads sharply down and rightward from there. That would mean higher taxes go together with lower standards of living. But

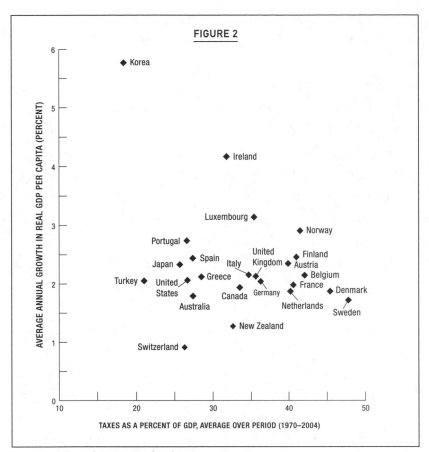

FIGURE 2

Source: Joel Slemrod, University of Michigan

there is no pattern like this at all. Some wealthy nations, like the United States and Japan, have relatively lower taxes (less than 30 percent of GDP), but others, particularly Scandinavian countries, have incomes nearly as high or in some cases higher than ours, with taxes of 45 or 50 percent of GDP.

So taxes seem to have no real effect on income levels. But what about their effect on economic growth over longer periods? As you can see, figure 2 compares the tax levels of many countries with how fast they've grown over the last three decades. Some low tax nations, like South Korea, did terrifically over this period, and some high tax countries, like Sweden, did relatively poorly. But the low tax United States performed *below* average. And a number of countries with higher taxes than ours had better long-term growth rates, including Austria, Finland, Norway, the United Kingdom, Luxembourg, and Ireland.

Research by Peter Lindert, an economic historian at the University of California, Davis, confirms these findings over longer periods. "Nine decades of historical experience fail to show that transferring a larger share of GDP from taxpayers to transfer recipients has a negative correlation with either the level or the rate of growth of GDP per person," he writes in *Growing Public,* a major study published in 2004. "The average correlation is essentially zero." Lindert notes further that by the late 1990s, a number of European countries had actually caught up to the United States in output per labor hour despite their higher taxes and spending as well. (Output per hour is a more accurate measure of labor productivity than output per person, since in Europe, workers work fewer hours each year).

"There's just no question that higher income countries have higher taxes," Michigan's Joel Slemrod says. "Now, what that tells about causation is not clear. But what it clearly tells us is that high taxes are by no means the kiss of death." Slemrod recalls a trip he took to Sweden right after he completed graduate school at Harvard, where he studied under the legendary conservative economist Martin Feldstein. "When I stepped off the airplane in Stockholm for the first time, I sort of expected to see the Stone Age," he says with a laugh. "Yet they're doing quite well. They've managed to find a way to have significantly more extensive government and more taxes than we do, and keep step prosperity-wise."

THIS IS NOT SWEDEN—
REPEAT, THIS IS NOT SWEDEN

Let's write this in neon: *no one is saying American taxes and spending will rise (or need to rise) to Scandinavian levels.* But the reassuring news, which is utterly absent in our political debate, is that even if they did, the experience of other countries shows that this is perfectly consistent with a thriving economy. Despite passionate arguments to the contrary, history and current experience show that social spending and the taxes that fund it have not materially weakened economic incentives and growth. How can that be?

For starters, the higher spending made possible by higher taxes often contributes to economic growth. Good schools, government-sponsored basic research, and high quality systems of health care, for example, make a nation's citizens more productive.

In addition, it turns out that high-spending welfare states have tax structures that are more pro-growth than those of the lower spending, lower tax countries. These nations seem to realize that if they're going to tax more, they'd better be extra careful to do so in ways that don't kill the golden goose of the economy. They therefore rely more on consumption taxes (like the VAT) and "sin" taxes on addictive substances like alcohol, tobacco, and gasoline, and less on corporate taxes or double taxation of dividends. It may seem paradoxical to American ears that higher tax countries are actually *smarter* about taxes than we are, but if you think about it for a moment, it makes perfect sense, because the stakes of getting the tax balance correct are so high. Moreover, the higher tax countries tend to be more open economies, meaning that trade comprises a greater share of their GDP; with their firms exposed to more international competition, their operations, and thus the economy broadly, become more efficient.

Assuring a strong economy even as taxes rise means getting other things right as well. For example, the restrictions many European countries place on the ability of firms to fire workers makes companies understandably cautious about hiring them in the first place. These "labor market restrictions" help explain why Europe has shown so little job growth in recent decades (and why it has high unemployment) while American job creation remains the envy of the world. Conservatives often try to lump together the prospect of higher taxes with these wrongheaded labor market approaches and dismiss the whole supposed package as "the discredited European model." But this criticism misses the point. America doesn't have to adopt Europe's ideas about labor markets; and our inevitably higher taxes, especially if implemented wisely (we'll discuss how in chapter 10), simply won't hurt overall growth.

Some leading conservative thinkers acknowledge at least parts of this macro story. I asked Kevin Hassett, the director of economic policy studies at the American Enterprise Institute and an adviser to John McCain's presidential campaign, what the impact would be if we shifted health care costs from business payrolls to government, and raised taxes by the same amount to accommodate the transfer of responsibility. "If in one of these scenarios we call the health expenditure 'government' and [in] the other we don't," he said, "what does it matter?" He added: "It's hard to imagine [that] that would have the [negative] growth effects" normally ascribed to tax increases in the economics literature.

BRAND MANAGEMENT

In general, however, when it comes to taxes, the conservative mind is caught in the past. Republicans cherish the political triumphs their tax cut mantra has delivered, and naturally resist the idea that its time is passing. But, as Ronald Reagan often said (quoting John Adams), "Facts are stubborn things." Lowering the top marginal tax rate from 70 percent toward 30 percent, as the Republicans did under Reagan, was a major economic and political achievement. Going downward from the mid-thirties, where the rate stands today, wouldn't be nearly as big a deal, and the boomers' imminent retirement makes it a moot question anyway.

So why does tax cutting mania persist among Republicans, I asked Douglas Holtz-Eakin, the McCain adviser—given that the impact can't be great at today's much lower tax rates, and that, as Holtz-Eakin himself explained to me, taxes will soon have to go up substantially in any event?

"It's the brand," he said. "And you don't dilute the brand."

The moral of the story? We've reached a moment in the history of American capitalism where our reflexive "Me-Tarzan-you-Jane-taxes-bad" mind-set is one of the biggest obstacles to pragmatically positioning the American economy for success in a global era.

There's been a kind of unwritten law since the 1950s under which taxes hover between 18 and 19 percent of GDP. When they inch higher, pressures seem to build to cut them. This pattern is sometimes cited as proof that the American people, in their mystical wisdom, won't tolerate taxes above this norm. The problem is that this metaphorical iron law is about to collide with the real iron law of mathematics, and the metaphor will have to give. Just as wars permanently altered the level of taxes and spending in the past, so will a lesser national emergency—the baby boomers' retirement, along with efforts to strengthen the safety net for the nonelderly in an age of rising economic anxiety—soon force taxes to new levels as well. This won't mean we become Sweden or France. And the economy, as all evidence suggests, will be fine.

"There's a broad-based understanding among experts who follow this that there's no way that we're going to be able to maintain tax levels at 18 to 19 percent of GDP," says David Walker, the former comptroller general. "The only question is: what higher level of taxation will we go to, when, and how are we going raise the related revenues?"

5

SCHOOLS ARE A LOCAL MATTER

In which we find that America's unique obsession
with local control and funding of education is sinking us
morally and economically

It wasn't just the slate and pencil on every desk, or the absence of
daily beatings. As Horace Mann sat in a Berlin classroom in the summer of 1843, it was his impression of the entire Prussian system of
schools that overwhelmed him. Mann, six years into the work as Massachusetts secretary of education that would earn him lasting fame
as the "father of public education," had sailed from Boston to England several weeks earlier. He was combining a European honey-
moon with educational fact finding. In England, the couple had been
startled by the luxury and refinement of the upper classes, which
exceeded anything they had seen in America and stood in stark contrast to the poverty and ignorance of the masses. If the United States
was to avoid this awful chasm and the social upheaval it seemed sure
to spawn, Mann thought, education was the answer. Now he was seeing firsthand the Prussian schools that were the talk of education
reformers on both sides of the Atlantic. What Mann saw shook his
longtime faith in America's destined leadership in human affairs.

In Massachusetts, Mann had to coax and cajole local districts of wildly varying quality. His vision of "common schools," publicly funded and attended by all, represented an inspiring democratic advance over the state's existing hodgepodge of privately funded and charity schools. But beyond using the bully pulpit, Mann had little power as a state official to make his vision a reality. Prussia, by contrast, was a system designed from the center. School attendance was compulsory. Teachers were trained at national institutes with the same care that went into training Prussian military officers, and they were "the finest collection of men I have ever seen," Mann wrote. The teachers' enthusiasm for their subjects was contagious, and their devotion to students evoked reciprocal affection and respect, making Boston's routine resort to classroom whippings seem barbaric. Mann also admired Prussia's rigorous national curriculum for each grade, tied to a system of national testing for all students. The results spoke for themselves; in Prussia, illiteracy had been vanquished, and a sense of national unity instilled. In Massachusetts, where such matters as teachers, textbooks, curriculum, and time in school were subject to the whims (and variable talents) of fickle town committees, some students prospered, while many languished. To be sure, Prussian schools sought to create obedient subjects who revered the king—hardly Mann's educational aim. Yet the lessons were undeniable. Mann returned home determined to share what he had seen, even if it hurt feelings and inflamed educators. In the seventh of his legendary "Annual Reports" on education to the Commonwealth of Massachusetts (reports which still read remarkably well today), Mann touted the benefits of a "national system . . . in which the whole people can participate" and warned against the "calamities which result . . . from leaving this most important of all the functions of a government to chance." Mann's message, according to his biographer, Jonathan Messerli, was clear:

The United States had fallen behind the Prussians in education, and in order to catch up and move ahead, it was now mandatory to create a truly professional corps of teachers, produce a systematic curriculum, and develop a more centralized and efficient supervision of the schools. The Prussians offered a model in practicality and efficiency which his own countrymen would be well advised to follow. This was his prescription and he desperately hoped it would be accepted while there was still time.

Mann's epiphany that summer—that a strong role for the central government was essential if America was to "accelerate the agenda of the Almighty" and use the power of education to lift all children, not just those favored by birth and circumstance—put him on the wrong side of America's tradition of radical localism when it came to schools. And while Mann's importunings in the years that followed made Massachusetts a model of taxpayer-funded schools and state-sponsored teacher training, this obsession with "local control" of education—so unlike the approach that most wealthy nations take for granted—pervades U.S. schooling to this day. Of all the hackneyed applause lines politicians proffer, few are more foolproof than to rail against "Washington bureaucrats" out to meddle with what communities and parents know best. "So deeply ingrained in our consciousness is the idea of 'local control of education' that few Americans even think about it anymore," says Chester E. Finn, Jr., a former Reagan administration education official who now runs the Thomas B. Fordham Foundation. "Like 'separation of church and state,' 'civilian control of the military,' and 'equality of opportunity,' the phrase rolls off the tongue without ever engaging the mind."

To be sure, for much of the 150 or so years between Mann's era and now, the system served us adequately; during that time we extended more schooling to more people than any nation had before and rose to superpower status. But let's look at what the idea of "local control" gives us today, in the world in which our students will have to compete.

The United States spends more than nearly every other wealthy nation on schools, yet out of twenty-nine developed countries participating in a 2003 assessment, America ranked twenty-fourth in math, twenty-fourth in problem solving, eighteenth in science, and fifteenth in reading—bested by such countries as Singapore and South Korea, which a few decades ago were considered hopelessly backward. One in two minority students in America doesn't graduate from high school on time (or at all). Seventy percent of American eighth graders are not proficient in reading. By the end of eighth grade, what passes for a math curriculum here is two years behind the math being studied in other countries. A 2003 test called "Problem Solving for Tomorrow's World" gave fifteen-year-olds real-life problems that involved decision making and troubleshooting—things like using a map to plan a trip, coordinating schedules to see a movie with friends, and the like. Among twenty-nine developed countries, the United States had the fourth highest percentage of weak problem solvers and the sixth lowest percentage of strong ones, placing us behind Latvia, Hungary, and Slovakia. Meanwhile, thanks to localized sources of school funding, the gap between what is spent in wealthy states and districts and in poorer ones routinely tops $5,000 per pupil. As a result, America systematically assigns the worst teachers and most run-down facilities in the country to the poor children who need great schools the most. In addition, most schools, far from relishing the supposed freedom granted by local control, feel trapped in red tape; principals say they spend their days on unproductive paperwork to comply with endless mandates, when they're not busy navigating byzantine district bureaucracies to keep the heat on and the supply room stocked.

If you thought President Bush's "No Child Left Behind" legislation, enacted with bipartisan fanfare in 2002, meant that Uncle Sam has stepped in to fix these woes, you're mistaken. NCLB requires states to establish standards in core subjects and test children annually to measure improvement in grades three to eight, with the aim of making all students "proficient" by 2014. Yet by leaving standards and the definition of "proficiency" entirely to state discretion, NCLB has sparked a race to dumb down requirements to create the illusion of progress. The result is a phony accountability regime built on quicksand. (Mississippi, for example, says that 89 percent of its fourth grade students are "proficient" in reading, while the respected National Assessment of Educational Progress says the level is 18 percent.) Nor does NCLB do anything to remedy the shocking financial inequities that plague education in America.

In the twenty-five years since the landmark study *A Nation at Risk* sounded the alarm about educational mediocrity, America's strategy, if it can be called that, has been dictated by some fifteen thousand school districts, with help more recently from the fifty states. It's as if Franklin Roosevelt had said we could put the U.S. economy on a war footing after Pearl Harbor by relying on the uncoordinated efforts of thousands of small factories; they'd know what kind of planes and tanks were needed, right? The results have been predictable. Despite pockets of improvement, we have made virtually no progress in raising the achievement of most students to the levels now required if Americans are to have a fighting chance in the coming era of competition with hungry workers in places like China and India.

There has to be a better way—and there is, if we open our minds. A look at the history of local control as the organizing principle of schooling suggests that an approach that made perfect sense in the eighteenth century is crippling American education today. For our children to thrive, we'll need finally to jettison the idea that Horace Mann was wise enough to look beyond in his own time: the anachronistic, damaging, and uniquely American notion that schools are simply a local matter.

LOCAL CONTROL: THE BACKSTORY

Local control began as the commonsense and even progressive way to organize and fund schools in the United States, so organic and straightforward an arrangement that there really wasn't need for much debate. The story begins in colonial New England, when education was a casual affair, left to parents, churches, and employers to arrange. Many children attended so-called dame schools, run by single women who hung out a shingle and offered their services teaching basic literacy and grammar. As towns grew in size, it became clear that voluntary arrangements wouldn't suffice to teach all children, as many parents neglected their duties. The Massachusetts Bay Colony established the right of the government to promote universal literacy in 1642, and followed with another measure in 1647, under which the colonial government, as servant of the church, required local townships with more than fifty families to school the young. The idea, embodied in law, was to combat "that Old Deluder, Satan," who was apparently out to keep people ignorant of scripture.

This link between religion and education explains much about the early history of American schools. Many of the groups that came to the United States, particularly in New England, were dissenters from centralized religious authority. For the Pilgrims, Puritans, and Quakers, the idea of having some ecclesiastical boss, whether he be in Canterbury or Rome, was what they were rebelling against. "Schooling in the seventeenth and eighteenth century was essentially literacy, which is a deeply Protestant enterprise," says Jeff Mirel, an historian of education at the University of Michigan. "To be able to read the Bible in the vernacular, to be able to make your own decisions without a pope or some other authority telling you what you have to believe, is ingrained in the Protestant tradition." The way religion and schooling moved in tandem across New England and into the mid-Atlantic colonies typically involved a group of people gathering in the community and setting up a church. If people didn't like the way the minister there was preaching, they moved on to another community and founded their own church, and generally their own school. Local control reflected parents' natural concern for how religious doctrines would be passed on to their children.

In the political realm, the American Revolution supplied a similar animating impulse: distrust of distant, centralized power. This doesn't mean a national role in education wasn't discussed. John Adams spoke eloquently about the need for a national system of some kind; George Washington floated the idea of a national university. For the founders, the potential lure of a national system was as a vehicle, in Benjamin Rush's phrase, to "unlearn" old ways of thinking associated with the imperial British. But in the end, the deeper consensus on the virtues of decentralized power carried the day. When it came time to draft the Constitution, education was left out; it is one of the unnamed powers reserved for the states in the Tenth Amendment, and the states in turn devolved this power to local communities.

America's rural geography and frontier mentality made such localism seem natural. As people moved west they got together and said "Let's build a school." Even in eastern states, once you settled over the hill or across the river, the idea that folks on the other side would have a say in how you taught your kids felt wrong. Eventually the United States would have 130,000 one-room schools. These little red schoolhouses, literally districts unto themselves, became the iconic symbols of democratic American learning.

MIND CONTROL

Yet local control set America apart from other nations. The French revolutionaries in the 1790s felt they had to revamp schooling because it had been ecclesiastically controlled. If the French were to become good republican citizens, the thinking went, they needed to have a national system of education, which in one form or another the French have run from Paris ever since. Their schemes were intrusive, to say the least. A 1793 law required that all children attend a boarding school from age five until age fifteen, in which they would be dressed alike in clothes provided by the state, fed the same food, and taught to be loyal only to the Republic. (The law was only sporadically implemented.) François Guizot, a senior minister under King Louis Philippe in the 1830s, wrote that every French village would be governed by a gendarme and a schoolteacher; the cop to control their bodies, the teacher to control their minds. "We didn't have a revolution like the French or the Russians did," says the historian Carl Kaestle of Brown University, "where it was such a social upheaval that governments took seriously the idea that you'd really have to retrain the population and run the schools."

Nor did the United States face at this point the same pressures to define exactly who was an American. In the early nineteenth century, France, Spain, and Prussia were wrestling to define themselves in the face of external enemies and internal divisions. Leaders feared that regions within their borders, which often spoke different languages and had little day-to-day awareness of the king, were going their own way. A national school system was a way to instill loyalty and to control the population through the minds of its children. In the United States, this sentiment appeared only late in the century, when immigration became heavy, giving rise, at least in big cities where immigrants gathered, to the idea that public schools were the place to "Americanize" the mob.

Slavery meant that the evolution of public education in the South would be a longer and more complicated matter, but by the decades after the Civil War the basic contours of local control were in place across the country. It is a bit jarring, given today's politics, to note that it was the "big government" Whigs and later the Republicans in the mid-nineteenth century who wanted more centralized authority over schools, part of a broader agenda that included government support for such infrastructure as canals and railroads. Democrats resisted this idea mightily, partly out of fears, especially in the South, that it would ultimately threaten the institution of slavery, and partly out of the Democrats' general conviction (like that of many Republicans today) that limited government served democracy best. This explains why Horace Mann and others who sought an expanded state role took care to pitch their reforms in ways that respected the primacy of local control.

Between 1825 and 1860, as the "common school" movement gained ground, two critical features of local control appeared that shape education today. The first was the emergence of independently elected school boards to administer schools apart from the rest of local government, with the power to raise taxes, hire and fire teachers and principals, choose textbooks, and the like. The second was the use of local property taxes as the primary funding mechanism for schools. School control was initially vested in towns, but as people moved farther from town centers, they wanted their own independent schools, and rather than stay subject to town authority, they formed small new school governing boards. A Massachusetts law ratifying this pragmatic decentralization became a model for other states as people moved west. Common school promoters also feared that linking schools to city or town governments could open the door to partisan efforts to "educate" kids into a specific ideology. In such a situation, support for the schools might erode as parents from the other party would remove their children or oppose funding the institution. Mann, for example, was adamant about keeping schools out of partisan politics for precisely these reasons. (This concern blossomed into a more sweeping Progressive drive early in the twentieth century to remove urban school districts from the corrupting influence of "politics," leaving them led by more "neutral" professional experts, with nonpartisan school boards picked in elections held at different times than regular elections.) Meanwhile, the property tax, now a chief source of inequity, was then considered the fairest way to pay for education. Property was the main form of wealth; rich and poor people did not live in separate taxing communities. "Thus the wealthy paid more than the middle class and the poor paid nothing," says the historian Jeff Mirel, "yet all got access to the same public service—public schools."

I'M FROM WASHINGTON AND I'M HERE TO HELP

Once the system of local control rooted in taxation and governance from the bottom up became sacrosanct (with a thin layer of state supervision above it), it faced only a few significant challenges in the late nineteenth and early twentieth centuries. While these challenges didn't prevail, the clash of ideas they elicited foreshadows the debates that are destined to be joined in the next few years.

The first flurry of activity came after the Civil War, during the period of Radical Reconstruction, when some in Congress, emboldened by the passage of the Thirteenth, Fourteenth, and Fifteenth amendments, sought to put educational flesh on these new constitutional guarantees of citizenship. A federal department of education was established in 1867, which, though downgraded to a mere data-collecting "office" in the Department of the Interior soon afterward, signaled a new sense that the federal government had a role to play. Then, in 1870, George Hoar, a Massachusetts congressman who had been a fierce foe of slavery, offered an unpredecented bill "to establish a system of national education." It required each state to provide instruction to children between the ages of six and eighteen in reading, writing, math, geography, and U.S. history. The president was authorized to determine whether each state had set up "a system of common schools that provides reasonably" in this regard; if not, the bill called for "national schools" run by a federal commissioner of education to fill the gap. The feds would select textbooks, build schools on land acquired by eminent domain, and pay for it all with a new federal tax of fifty cents per person.

According to Goodwin Liu, a law professor at Berkeley who has written the best modern account of these debates, Hoar's bill was attacked as "a system of functionaryism" sure to bring "reckless expenditure" and "patronage." Letting the feds pick textbooks was a means by which "the very foundations of knowledge might be poisoned," critics roared. Yet Hoar made his case with equal passion. "Now, if to every man in every State is secured by national authority his equal share in the Government," he said, "surely there is implied the corresponding power and duty of securing *the capacity of the exercise* of that share in the Government" (emphasis added). Hoar underscored that his measure was not aimed merely at newly freed blacks; whites accounted for half of America's illiterates, after all, and there were twice as many school-aged white children who did not attend school as there were black children. "What then, is the function of the national Legislature?" he asked. "It is twofold. It is to compel to be done what the States will not do, and to do for them what they cannot do . . . either through indifference, hostility to education, or pecuniary inability." The bill died without a vote, sunk finally by suspicions that the federal government would also seek to compel racial integration in schools.

Hoar lost, but he made an impression. In 1872, Representative Legrand Perce, a Mississippi Republican, offered a less heavy-handed plan that would help address the nation's emerging education gaps: dedicate half the annual revenue from sales of federal lands to a permanent "national education fund," with the other half going directly in aid to states that provided free schooling to children. It would allocate money to states on the basis of their illiteracy levels (offering some aid to all regions, therefore, but targeting the South), with the proviso that the states spend the money on teachers. The proposal specified that states would not lose funding if their schools were not racially mixed. Perce's more pragmatic bill passed the House with bipartisan support before being quashed in the Senate. Still, the effort suggested that crafting a politically acceptable federal role to offset the shortcomings of local control was not necessarily a pipe dream. In 1875, President Ulysses S. Grant even proposed a constitutional amendment under which "the States shall be required to afford the opportunity of a good common school education to every child within their limits."

The culmination of these postwar federal challenges to local control came in the 1880s, when Senator Henry Blair of New Hampshire proposed that new federal school aid to the states be made from general appropriations, not from public lands. The Blair bill actually passed the Senate in 1884, 1886, and 1888 before failing, thanks to parliamentary machinations, in 1890. The fights over the Blair measure cover hundreds of pages in the *Congressional Record*, which include detailed statistics highlighting gross inequities across the states. The per capita value of real and personal property in New England, for example, where student enrollment was high and illiteracy rates low, was 40 percent greater than in the mid-Atlantic states, twice as high as in the Midwest and West, and fully four times greater than in the South, where enrollment rates were low and illiteracy rates high. Reflecting these difference in fiscal capacity, New Englanders spent three or four times more per pupil than southerners. Blair argued that the federal government had "the duty of educating the people of the United States whenever for any cause these people are deficient in the degree of education which is essential to the discharge of their duties as citizens." By allocating aid based on illiteracy rates in each state, he envisioned a role for the federal government in offsetting interstate inequities in both finance and educational outcomes. Though in the end Blair and his allies failed to overcome the usual fears of a school takeover by the wasteful feds, they anticipated by eighty years the approach to augmenting local control that would be enacted by Lyndon Johnson.

WISE GUYS

Similar seeds were planted in 1894 when "the Committee of Ten," chaired by Charles Eliot, the president of Harvard University, issued a report on "Secondary School Subjects" that educators viewed as the most important educational document ever issued in the United States. Eliot's committee also included the presidents of the universities of Michigan, Missouri, and Colorado, along with W. T. Harris, the U.S. commissioner of education and the former schools chief in St. Louis. The group's charge was to review high school curricula and to propose requirements for admission to college. Their recommendations set off a fierce twenty-year debate whose shadow still hangs over us today.

The Committee of Ten's radical argument was that every high school student, regardless of background and "probable destiny," should have a rigorous liberal arts college preparatory education. "They were the first to essentially call for some kind of nationalization of the high school curriculum," says Jeff Mirel.

This idea was viewed by progressive educators as elitist, for it ignored the supposedly lower aptitudes and abilities of the immigrant children flooding the schools. Preparation for college, Progressives argued, was not for everyone, and was not the same thing as preparation for life. Why should a child be studying calculus when he's going to be a factory worker? Why does he have to read *Hamlet* when he's going to be a carpenter? The committee's critics believed that if you pushed college prep, kids who were unwilling or unable to do the work would get frustrated and drop out. They needed constructive options suited to their station in life. The result was a furious backlash against Eliot and his colleagues, and the successful push to create the "comprehensive" high school, with its college prep track, yes, but also with major tracks for vocational, general, and commercial education, which to some extent are with us still.

What made the debate fascinating was that both sides believed they were the true apostles of equal educational opportunity. To the Committee of Ten, equality was about the abolition of tracking and the achievement of higher standards for all. To the Progressives, it was about a chance to excel in different ways particular to the kind of person you were. The Progressives also stressed a practical challenge: How do you keep these less academic kids in school? School needs to have more entertainment value, they thought. It's not the content of what they learn so much as the credential they'll have that will enable these children to move up in society.

To make a long story short, the Progressives won this pedagogical fight for the twentieth century, until *A Nation at Risk* shattered America's complacency in 1983 and sparked the standards-based reform movement that represents the latest (if still ineffectively meek) challenge to local control. Meanwhile, the challenge sidestepped a century ago—how to raise *all* students, not just a few, to higher levels of achievement—is newly urgent in an era of global competition, when, as Bill Clinton's refrain goes, "What you can earn depends on what you can learn."

NO CHARADE LEFT BEHIND

It's short work to bring the saga of local control up to the present. After World War II, liberals in Congress tried again to aid poorer states and localities, but couldn't make headway thanks to the three Rs: race, religion, and reds. The South didn't want Congress forcing integration down its throat. Increasingly powerful Catholic constituencies resisted the idea that aid would go to public schools but not to parochial schools. Then there were suspicions that the federal bureaucracy harbored communists. Only after *Brown v. Board of Education,* Sputnik, and the civil rights movement was there sufficient momentum for President Lyndon Johnson to pass legislation offering federal aid to poor districts in 1965, followed by similar initiatives for children with disabilities and other special needs.

At the same time, the postwar era saw the appearance of new and dramatic funding differences between school districts in the same state. The culprit was the commuter suburb. The suburban building boom made it possible for people to self-select communities based on wealth. The dirty little secret of local control became the enormous tax advantage it conferred on better-off Americans; communities with high property wealth could tax themselves at lower rates and generate far more dollars per pupil than could poorer communities taxing themselves at higher rates. As advocates for the poor came to appreciate this situation, a legal movement emerged to challenge school finance systems, which left dozens of states facing court orders to help poorer communities do better. Over time this improved things, but only marginally; today local taxes still represent 44 percent of school funding nationally, with states contributing 47 percent and the federal government 9 percent.

Meanwhile, the standards movement spawned by *A Nation at Risk* produced well-meaning commitments but glacial change. A Charlottesville summit of governors in 1989, which was keynoted by President George H. W. Bush (and in which Governor Bill Clinton of Arkansas played a leading role), committed to ambitious education goals for the year 2000. Yet Bush, torn between his view that the federal government now needed to take a stronger role and his conservative base's loathing of the idea, offered little beyond gestures to advance the cause. As president, Clinton repackaged Bush's toothless efforts and for a time put serious political capital into expanding the federal government's educational reach. But his attempts to promote even voluntary versions of national standards went nowhere.

Which brings us to No Child Left Behind. Seen in the light of history, the major accomplishment of the law, which liberal critics don't appreciate, is the way it committed the modern Republican Party to an expanded federal role in schooling—a return, as it were, to the party's roots in the nineteenth century. This is no mean feat when you recall that it wasn't so long ago that Ronald Reagan and Newt Gingrich were pledging to abolish the Department of Education altogether. Moreover, by requiring schools to "dis-aggregate" their reporting of test scores, so that local districts can no longer hide the dismally lagging performance of minority children, NCLB has shone a sharper light on the "achievement gap." President George W. Bush deserves credit for these steps, but they're modest compared to education's woes. "It has the veneer of a toothy federal intervention," says Chris Cerf, the deputy schools chancellor in New York City, "but there's not a whole lot behind it." Adds Andrew Rotherham, a former Clinton education official who now serves on the school board of the state of Virginia: "NCLB is the beginning of a long national conversation about aggregating some of this decision-making at a national level."

SO LET'S TALK

The question is where the conversation should go from here. In order to answer intelligently, it's important to have an honest accounting of the problems local control has caused. The system's defenders have inertia and political power on their side; public officials who know how harmful local control is fear speaking out because it can be a career ender. Foundations and advocacy groups who judge it prudent to be able to work with school boards also pull their punches. But we'll never get past make-believe fixes without speaking the truth. How does local control damage American education? Let us catalogue the ways:

SHOCKING FINANCIAL INEQUITY. "Some of the worst places in the country are in Chicago, or Michigan, or Pennsylvania, where you can go to an inner city and see a facility that's just horribly run down, where they're spending $6,000 a kid," says Tom Vander Ark, a former superintendent of schools in Tacoma, Washington, who from 1999 to 2006 ran the education program at the Bill and Melinda Gates Foundation. "You can drive twenty minutes down the street and see a spectacular facility where they're spending two and a half times as much per student. We should be spending more on low income kids to improve their educational experience and outcomes, and we do the opposite, and that's entirely a product of local control."

As it turns out, spending gaps *between* states (as opposed to *within* states) actually account for the greatest share of financial inequity across the nation. Even after adjusting for regional cost differences and varying student needs, one study shows that the top ten states ranked by per pupil spending invest nearly 50 percent more per student than the lowest ranking ten states, a difference of more than $2,500 per pupil. As was the case after the Civil War, the lower spending southern and western states still tend, generally speaking, to have the lowest achievement rankings as well. And Title I, the federal aid program meant to boost poor schools, actually makes these gaps worse, because it distributes money largely based on how much states are already spending. The result is that Uncle Sam perversely makes rich states richer. "In the developed countries, there's no school system funded as inequitably as the United States," says Sir Michael Barber, a former education adviser to the British prime minister Tony Blair, who now consults to school officials around the world. Marc Tucker, who led the New

Commission on the Skills of the American Workforce (a bipartisan blue-ribbon panel that called for a bold overhaul of the system), puts it this way:

> The commission could not figure out how we would ever have a high performing education system as long as we permit the wealthiest people among us to congregate in their own taxing districts, thereby producing very high budgets per student . . . at very low tax rates for themselves, and gaining the very best resources, including the best teachers available to any students in the state. When you put it to people that way, it makes them scratch their heads.

NO GOOD INFORMATION ON HOW CHILDREN ARE DOING.   "We're fifteen years into the standards movement in this country," says Tom Vander Ark, "and standards are still different by classroom, by school, by district, and by state." He continues:

> That's unquestionably a residual of local control. It's not just that every district sets their own standards, but the fact that every district has had to structure their own employment agreements, which has basically kept administrators out of the classrooms [as observers] in a lot of places. Teachers in America still pretty much teach whatever they want. And even with the movement towards state standards, every state has a different set of standards, and then districts within a state have a different set of standards. It's just such a mess.

"The Proficiency Illusion," a report released in late 2007 by the conservative Thomas B. Fordham Foundation, makes clear what a charade the standards regime has become under NCLB. "'Proficiency' varies wildly from state to state," the report finds, "with 'passing scores' ranging from the 6th percentile to the 77th. . . . It's not just that results vary, but that they vary almost randomly, errat-ically, from place to place and grade to grade and year to year in ways that have little or nothing to do with student achievement." The report continues:

> Congress erred bigtime when NCLB assigned each state to set its own standards and devise and score its own tests; no matter what one thinks of America's history of state primacy in K–12 education, this study underscores the folly of a big modern nation, worried about its global competitiveness, nodding with approval as Wiscon-sin sets its eighth grade reading passing level at the 14th percentile while South Carolina sets it at the 71st percentile.

As a result, the report notes, "Susie may be 'proficient' in math in the eyes of Michigan education bureaucrats but she still could have scored worse than five-sixths of the other fourth graders in the country." In Massachusetts, a fourth grader demonstrates profi-ciency in reading by answering questions about a challenging pas-sage from a short story by Tolstoy; in Colorado, a proficient fourth grader tackles material that reads like *See Jane Run.*

"The lack of a simple national way to evaluate how all children are progressing is enormously anachronistic," say New York's Chris Cerf. "It is a reflection of this allegiance to localism. It allows this tremendous sense of delusion around how well children are doing."

NO R&D.   Local control has prevented education from attracting the research and development that accelerates progress in almost every other human endeavor. This is because the benefits from scale that drive such activities elsewhere are absent. There are fifteen thou-sand curriculum departments in the country, for example—one for every district. None of them can afford to invest in understanding at a deep level what works and doesn't work in, say, teaching reading to English language learners. Or consider the shabby state of learning technology. Outside the classroom, kids are constantly online or playing sophisticated video games; at the doctor's office they're diagnosed with cutting edge equipment. In school, by contrast, the core learning technology of a teacher and twenty-five or thirty kids in a room looks exactly as it did fifty years ago.

Why hasn't there been a massive R&D effort to understand (to cite but one possible example) how to use computers to develop customized reading-learning strategies for kids with different learning styles? Fifteen thousand school districts obviously can't take this on, yet the federal government would be damned for trying by the local control fetishists. Perhaps most important, the private sector won't pursue it either, because curriculum and education technology purchasing decisions are made in fifteen thousand fragmented little arenas. Ask anyone who tries to do business with school systems: when you have a long-term, highly decentralized, complicated, and difficult sale to try to make, it reduces the amount of product development and research in which private companies are willing to invest. A vendor in the United States can't produce a sophisticated learning platform and go to a school administrator and say, "I have a powerful new learning tool that can transform the experience of a hundred thousand or a million or five million young people." There's no one to have that conversation with in the United States. In South Korea and Singapore, there is.

UNION DOMINANCE. Local control essentially surrenders power over the way schools work to the teachers' unions, with whom local school boards can't compete. First of all, unions are often responsible for electing board members in low turnout elections in which union money and mobilization can dominate. But the unions also bring the intellectual and political horsepower of their state and national affiliates, which monitor contracts around the state and country and develop and spread successful negotiating strategies. Even when they're not in the unions' pockets, in other words, school boards are overmatched.

Unions have become adept at enacting improvements to local contracts, spreading them to other districts around a state, then getting them embodied in state policy, and to some extent in federal law as well. The result is an impenetrable three-tier set of policy mandates that is interlocked with employment agreements in ways that leave new superintendents operating with both hands tied behind their backs. It is extraordinarily difficult to make changes to staffing, compensation, employment policy, curriculum, or the length and schedule of the school day. Superintendents develop a kind of "learned helplessness" in the face of these obstacles, a sense that they have to live within a shrinking box. Meanwhile, common-sense reforms, such as higher pay to attract teachers to high-needs schools or to "shortage specialties" like math, science, or special education, can't get traction because the unions say no.

SCHOOL BOARD INCOMPETENCE AND DYSFUNCTION. "In the first place, God made idiots," said Mark Twain. "That was for practice. Then he made school boards." Times haven't changed much, though few educators will say so on the record. "The job has become more difficult, more complicated, and more political, and as a result, it's driven out many of the good candidates that no longer want to put in the time or suffer the sort of brain damage, the personal insult that comes with the job," says Tom Vander Ark. "So while teachers' unions have become more sophisticated and have smarter people who are better equipped and prepared at the table, the quality of school board members, particularly in urban areas, has decreased." A senior urban school official is blunter. After health care, he notes, education is the second largest sector in the United States, with upwards of half a trillion dollars spent annually. "The more distributed the authority over that money is, the more people can play," he says. "The kind of people who have been elected to run our school systems would never in any other world have the opportunity to control that big a piece of this huge pie."

Chester Finn, the former Reagan official, writes that school boards today "resemble a dysfunctional family comprised of three unlovable types: aspiring politicians for whom this is a stepping-stone to higher office, former school system employees with a score to settle, and single-minded advocates of diverse dubious causes who yearn to use the public schools to impose their particular hang-ups on all the kids in town." Once installed, these folks routinely spend their time on minor matters, from meddling in midlevel personnel decisions to tweaking bus routes. "The tradition goes back to the rural era that we started with," says Michael Kirst, a professor emeritus of education at Stanford University, "where the school board hired the schoolmarm and oversaw the repair of the roof, looked into the stove in the room, and deliberated on every detail of operating the schools. The L.A. School Board still does that." Thanks to the unintended consequence of Progressive Era reforms meant to get school boards out of "politics," most urban school districts became independent entities, beyond the reach of mayors and city councils. Elected in off-year races few people notice or vote in, school boards are, in effect, not accountable to anyone.

It may be that in the heyday of the common school movement in the nineteenth century, local school boards served as authentic, even romantic seats of small-d democracy in action. But that was then. Today, in the districts in which most American children go to school, school boards have instead been captured by a swarm of special interests, with employee groups, contractors, and other adults who do business with the district looking out for themselves while cynically proclaiming "It's all about the kids." Many reformers across the political spectrum agree that local control as currently practiced has become a disaster for our schools. Support for it lingers because of the natural default preference for having things done nearby, and because the case against local control is almost never articulated. Few people with political ambitions will take on the powerful defenders of the status quo and tell people the truth—including the truth that real autonomy and equity can be created for schools only by scrapping what we traditionally think of as "local control." For now, an idea that should have lost its grip on us long ago goes unchallenged. In the unfolding era of unprecedented global competition, millions of poorly prepared children will pay the price.

6

MONEY FOLLOWS MERIT

In which we see that the educated class's belief
in economic meritocracy is being shattered by
the rise of the undeserving rich

Not long ago an investment banker worth some $80 million told me that he wasn't in his line of work for the money. "If I was doing this for the money," he said, with no trace of irony, "I'd be at a hedge fund." What to say? Only on a small plot of real estate in lower Manhattan at the dawn of the twenty-first century could such a statement be remotely fathomable. That it is suggests how debauched our ruling class has become, which, at least since Marie Antoinette's day, usually portends all manner of unpleasantness.

The widening chasm between rich and poor threatens our democracy. But if that banker's lament staggers your brain as it did mine, you're on your way to seeing why the coming clash over America's income gap won't be some retro fight between "proletarians" and "capitalists." The new class war destined to shake up our society will be fought between what I call the "lower upper class" and the ultrarich. And it will be launched because of a Dead Idea.

My theory is that economic resentment at the bottom of the top 1 percent of America's income distribution is the new wild card in public life. Ordinary workers never rise up against Ultras because they take it as given that "the rich get richer." But the most cherished illusion of a certain sliver of today's educated class is that market capitalism is a meritocracy.

Hence the psychic turmoil of the Lower Uppers. You know them as doctors, accountants, engineers, and lawyers. At companies they're mostly executives above the rank of vice president but below the CEO. Lower Uppers are professionals who by dint of schooling, hard work, and luck are living better than 99 percent of the humans who have ever walked the planet. They're also people who can't help but notice how many folks with credentials like theirs seem to be living in the kind of Gatsbyesque splendor they'll never enjoy—and squeezing them out of prerogatives they've long taken for granted.

This stings. If people no smarter or better than you are making $10 or $50 or $100 million, while you're working yourself ragged to scrape by on a million or two—or, God forbid, a couple hundred thousand—then something must be wrong. You can hear the fallout in conversations in office towers and tony suburbs across the country. A New York–based market research guru—a well-to-do fellow who has built and sold his own firm—explodes in a rant about Ultras bidding up real estate prices. A doctor in Los Angeles with two kids shakes his head and explains that between tuition and donations, Ultras have raised the ante for private school slots to the point where he can't get his kids enrolled. A senior executive at a nationally known firm seethes at the idea of eliminating the estate tax; it's an Ultra conspiracy in his view, a giveaway to people whose outsized lucre bears little relation to hard work. As one civic-minded Lower Upper businessman told me, even his charitable contributions now feel insignificant: when buyout kings plunk down a million a year for youth or arts groups, his $20,000 contribution doesn't get him the right to cochair a dinner, let alone a seat on the board. There's only so much of this indignity a vocal, powerful elite can take before the seams burst and a bilious reaction against unmerited privilege starts oozing from every pore—especially when it's clear to Lower Uppers that many Ultras are not simply reaping the rewards of the "free market," but are benefiting from rigged compensation systems in boardrooms and on Wall Street that are as likely to reward mediocrity as success.

To be sure, it's hard to get too worked up about the "suffering" of the Lower Uppers. Given their affluence, their complaints can seem spoiled and unsympathetic, their whining like the warbling of a tiny, exotic breed. Yet their perceptions and attitudes matter greatly to the rest of the country, because as a group, the 2 million or so Americans at the bottom of the top wield disproportionate influence. Lower Uppers hold important positions in industry, finance, government, media, and the professions. Today's Dead Ideas persist largely because of the faulty outlook of these elites; after all, if our culture is in the grip of old ways of thinking, who but our "opinion leaders" should bear the blame? Until they start thinking more clearly about the world we've entered, every American will pay the price.

This is why the current emotional crisis of the Lower Uppers isn't some niche sociological curiosity, but an opportunity for the country. The emergence of extreme inequality and the rise of the undeserving rich are shattering an idea that has long been at the core of the professional class's self-esteem. It's the idea that money follows "merit"—that in a system of market capitalism, people basically end up economically where they deserve to. What the Lower Uppers decide to do once they've realized that this isn't quite the case may well change the future for all of us.

THE MEEK SHALL INHERIT, REGARDLESS OF THEIR SATS

The notion of a close link between economic standing and moral dignity or overall status is relatively new. As Alain de Botton observes in his wonderful book, *Status Anxiety,* from the time of Christ up to the twentieth century, there were three credible and soothing narratives on offer that assured the poor or otherwise humble that they were no "worse" in an ultimate sense than anybody else. According to the first story, the poor were not responsible for their condition and were actually the most useful members of society. Premodern man believed that an individual's place in the social hierarchy was decided not by anything he did or didn't do, but by God. Despite vast differences in the lives of the nobility, the clergy, and the peasantry, there was nonetheless a strong sense of mutual dependence among them. As one medieval abbot wrote around the year 1015, wealth was created almost entirely by the poor, who rose early, toiled in the fields, and brought in the harvests. Each class depended on the others' playing their assigned roles; well-born children were raised to respect the hard lives endured by peasants in making agrarian economies work.

The second comforting story came straight from scripture: the New Testament preached that wealth and poverty were not measures of moral worth. Jesus, after all, had been poor, yet he was also the most blessed. As Christianity spread, the meek learned that they stood to inherit the earth, while the rich were told they had less hope of Heaven than did the camel of getting through the eye of that needle.

The third story was that the rich were sinful and corrupt and owed their wealth to their robbery of the poor. Social critics from Rousseau to Marx denounced the exploitation of the masses and assured those at the bottom that justice and revolution were coming. For twenty centuries these stories in one form or another offered solace for those not fated to be on top.

Yet very different stories gained ground after the eighteenth century to alter people's sense of their place in the world even as the Industrial Revolution raised their living standards. One new narrative held that the rich were in fact the useful ones, not the poor. The economic theorist Adam Smith argued that the spending of the wealthy, rather than being proof of damnable corruption and extravagance, was actually an engine of economic activity and employment. Unattractive as their showy consumption and grasping behavior might seem, the rich, not the poor, were the real economic heroes.

Next came the narrative that economic status *did* have moral connotations. It's hard to overstate the transformation this idea represented. Until this time, as de Botton writes,

> the assertion of a disjuncture between rank and intrinsic value was hard to refute when in Western societies positions had for centuries been distributed according to bloodlines and family connections rather than talent, a practice which had resulted in generations of kings who couldn't rule, lords who couldn't manage their own estates, commanders who didn't understand the intricacies of battle, peasants who were brighter than their masters and maids who knew more than their mistresses.

Starting in the eighteenth century, however, people began to question the hereditary principle. "I smile to myself when I contemplate the ridiculous insignificance into which literature and all the sciences would sink, were they made hereditary," wrote Thomas Paine in *The Rights of Man,* published in 1791, "and I carry the same idea into government. An hereditary governor is as inconsistent as an hereditary author." Napoleon, who loathed the "imbeciles and hereditary asses," agreed; he extended educational opportunity, made senior appointments without regard to birth or pedigree, and generally promoted his vision of "careers open to talents," an idea that survived his fall and inspired reformers everywhere. In Britain and the United States, these new impulses combined with Charles Darwin's theories to yield the ugly (but for rich people quite gratifying) philosophy of Social Darwinism, which held that life's economic race was simply another contest in which the fittest survived. For the winners—especially the self-made tycoons of America's Gilded Age—this philosophy was a double boon: it conferred a welcome sense of superiority even as it absolved the rich from any sense of obligation to aid the poor, since charity or government assistance would only sustain these sorry souls beyond the early demise ordained by their natural inferiority.

THE ASCENT OF MERIT

George Bernard Shaw was the most trenchant dissenter from these growing assertions of a link between money and merit. "Nothing hides the difference in merit between one person and another so much as differences in income," Shaw sallied in 1928 in *The Intelligent Woman's Guide to Socialism and Capitalism.*

> It is a monstrous thing that a man who, by exercising a low sort of cunning, has managed to grab three or four millions of money selling bad whisky, or forestalling the wheat harvest and selling it at three times its cost, or providing silly newspapers and magazines for the circulation of lying advertisements, should be honored and deferred to and waited on and returned to Parliament and finally made a peer of the realm, whilst men who have exercised their noblest faculties or risked their lives in the furtherance of human knowledge and welfare should be belittled by the contrast between their pence and the grabbers' pounds.
>
> Only where there is pecuniary equality can the distinction of merit stand out. Money [then] is nothing: character, conduct and capacity are everything. . . . [In a world of equal incomes] there would be great people and ordinary people and little people; but the great would always be those who had done great things, and never the idiots whose mothers had spoiled them and whose fathers had left them a hundred thousand a year; and the little

would be persons of small minds and mean characters, and not poor persons who never had a chance. That is why idiots are always in favor of inequality of income (their only chance of eminence), and the really great in favor of equality.

But Shaw's iconoclastic egalitarianism didn't catch on. Instead, in the United States, the harsh philosophy of Social Darwinism eventually yielded to a subtler, more pervasive and institutionally administered belief in meritocracy, and over time to the idea that those with "merit" would deservedly enjoy the best of society's material rewards.

Like many great social transitions, the move to enshrine meritocracy was well intended. In his superb history *The Big Test,* the journalist Nicholas Lemann tells how leaders like James Bryant Conant, the president of Harvard University, and Henry Chauncy, the intelligence testing pioneer who came to lead the Educational Testing Service, thought the clubby, inheritance-based American establishment of the 1930s and 1940s made a mockery of the nation's founding ideal of equal opportunity. They believed that widespread use of newly invented tests like the SAT would finally allow Thomas Jefferson's vision of an "aristocracy of talent" to be realized, under which, in Jefferson's words, "the best geniuses would be raked from the rubbish annually, and be instructed at public expense." These diamonds in the rough, unearthed by the SAT and whisked off to the Ivy League from far-flung farms and urban ghettos, would be cultivated for lives of public service, unconcerned with financial gain. That, at least, was the theory.

Over time this changed. The desire to diversify America's insular governing elite eventually led to a fetish for IQ-related aptitude tests and a national frenzy over college admissions as the arbiter of economic destinies. In the decades since World War II, these forces cumulatively altered the culture, creating among the winners a sense that their place in society, with all its financial and status rewards, was deserved. It is true that the elite chosen and nurtured by the new system included more women, minorities, and people from humble backgrounds than did the old boys' club. But there was always something amiss in the way the new meritocrats came to feel they "deserved" their position. Doing so meant ignoring the still vast discrepancies in people's starting places that assured that millions of poor children never had a chance to compete for the best colleges. The winners typically overlooked this reality, since it tended to undermine their sense of worthiness; the presence of a few remarkable children who rose against the odds to take a seat next to them in Harvard's classrooms assuaged any lingering discomfort they might have felt regarding the fact that the deck was mostly stacked in the winners' favor from the get-go.

All of which makes the psychic blow now being delivered by the new ultrarich deliciously ironic. Lower Uppers are being bitten by the sensibility that nourished them. The glorification of "merit," it turns out, has a profoundly threatening downside. In the old days, if you didn't end up on top, it didn't say anything about you personally. It was God's will; you were playing your role in the great chain of being; you'd get your reward in the next life. But now, if you're merely a corporate lawyer or a senior vice president of marketing in a world where your former classmates have private planes, something has to be wrong with *you*. Michael Young, the British socialist who coined the phrase "meritocracy" half a century ago to describe what he thought was a repulsive way to organize society, saw the comeuppance coming. "Today all persons, however humble, know they have had every chance," he wrote in 1958. "Are they not bound to recognize that they have an inferior status, not as in the past because they were denied opportunity, but because they *are* inferior?" Oscar Wilde anticipated Lower Upper angst as well. "Misfortunes one can endure, they come from outside, they are accidents," he once observed. "But to suffer for one's own faults— ah, there is the sting of life!"

THE ROT AT THE TOP

For many Lower Uppers the most egregious symbol of the growing disconnect between money and merit is CEO pay. Hardly a
month goes by without another shocking instance of failed corporate leaders being rewarded with astronomical wealth despite
abysmal performance. Consider Merrill Lynch and Citigroup.
Under the leadership of Stanley O'Neal and Charles Prince, respectively, these financial giants incurred more than $20 billion in losses
during the subprime mortgage fiasco. Thousands of employees
were fired as a result. Yet these men left their jobs with inexplicable
riches. Prince earned at least $120 million from running Citigroup
for four years, during which time $64 billion in company market
value vanished. O'Neal received a $161 million package when
ousted after presiding over the biggest losses in the firm's history.
For both men these jackpots came on top of the tens of millions
they had earned in previous years thanks largely to illusory gains
from mortgage-related businesses that were fated to implode.

Such stories are depressingly routine. Robert Nardelli walked
away from Home Depot with at least $250 million after a five-year
stint in which the stock value remained flat—and Home Depot's
board had the chutzpah afterward to refuse to answer any questions about this scandal at the company's annual meeting. Hank
McKinnell left the helm of Pfizer with nearly $200 million even
though Pfizer's market capitalization dropped by more than
$130 billion on his watch. Carly Fiorina put Hewlett Packard on
the ropes only to depart with $100 million. Gerald Levin earned
a stunning $600 million despite engineering the failed Time
Warner–AOL merger, which led the stock to drop from $58 to $9,
costing shareholders a cool $100 billion. Morgan Stanley executives
Philip Purcell and Stephen Crawford were ousted after a similar
performance. Their consolation prize? A hundred million dollars
on the way out.

It's all a far cry from the days when CEOs and boards of directors exhibited some sense of proportion and restraint. George Romney, who served as the CEO of American Motors in the 1950s, may be the most interesting example of this lost species. Romney voluntarily turned down $268,000 in pay over five years when he was CEO, which represented about 20 percent of his earnings over that period. "In 1960, for example," the *New York Times* noted, "he refused a $100,000 bonus. Mr. Romney had previously told the company's board that no executive needed to make more than $225,000 [about $1.4 million in today's dollars], a spokesman for American Motors explained at the time, and the bonus would have put him above that threshold." And this was a CEO who was performing well! Can anyone imagine Stanley O'Neal or Charles Prince turning back their undeserved bounty? That it seems unthinkable speaks volumes about the decline of ethical corporate leadership.

The defenders of today's CEO loot cite academic research purporting to show that compensation has risen appropriately in line with market sizes, global demands, and the potential for individual "stars" to add enormous value. But anyone familiar with the clubby world of board compensation committees and their consultants knows that CEO pay has nothing to do with the operation of the free market—it's a rigged system in which all forces conspire to push pay packages ever higher regardless of results. "I honestly don't understand why more CEOs aren't concerned about the image of business leaders in general," Edgar Woolard, the retired CEO of DuPont, told the *Times* in 2005. Woolard, who knows the game from the inside, calls all the fancy justifications of today's CEO pay "bull" and "double bull."

Some hedge fund compensation schemes raise similar questions, but at even more outsized levels. In 2007 the top fifty individual hedge find managers earned $29 billion, meaning their average income was twelve thousand times the income of the typical family. The top five alone earned $12.6 billion, which was equal to the combined pay of the lowest earning 9 million workers. In 2004 the top twenty-five hedge fund earners together took home more than the CEOs of the S&P 500 combined. Some of these investors performed terrifically. But a growing number benefit disproportionately from the classic hedge fund fee structure, under which the fund takes, off the top, 2 percent of all assets under management, and then adds 20 percent of the trading profits generated. Funds that attract large volumes of assets are often guaranteed excellent paydays before the managers even turn on their computers. And with pension funds, college endowments, and other institutional investors feeling increasingly compelled to chase higher returns via "alternative" investments (given the overall stock market's mixed outlook), these volumes are not as correlated to "superior performance" as hedge fund managers like to claim. Bridgewater Associates, based in Greenwich, Connecticut, earned a net return of less than 4 percent in 2006, but its founder, Raymond Dalio, pocketed $350 million nonetheless. "The combination of extraordinary pay and ordinary performance is going to occur more and more in coming years," concluded David Leonhardt of the *New York Times* after a review of industry trends.

I'VE GOT YOU UNDER MY SKIN

Not all Lower Uppers express resentment and frustration. One senior executive told me he's earning so much more than he dreamed he would when he was growing up that the greater wealth at the tippy-top doesn't bother him on a personal level. What worries him more is the way that executive compensation packages in, say, banking have created incentives for high risk behavior that produced a subprime meltdown that could threaten the whole economy. Lower Uppers I spoke with also routinely admired entrepreneurs who took risks to build businesses that add something valuable to society: no one begrudges Steve Jobs or Bill Gates their pile.

Still, that leaves plenty of undeserving rich getting under the skin of the Lower Uppers. The sociology of this brewing phenomenon is potentially explosive. The best performing gerbils on the treadmill of American meritocracy are learning that working hard, acing every test, attending top colleges, and succeeding in their chosen profession is no longer the path to the topmost ranks of wealth, influence, and respect in American society. They are also learning that the era ahead may leave their jobs increasingly vulnerable to competition and wage pressure from abroad (as tax accountants, radiologists, and divorce lawyers already know)—and this vulnerability is certainly *not* something Lower Uppers feel they "deserve." At the same time, Lower Uppers see that their "betters" routinely behave in ways that are startlingly selfish and corrupt, disqualifying them from playing any credible leadership role in society and leaving a vacuum increasingly filled by cynicism. Which brings us to a provocative question: If looking *above* now makes Lower Uppers bridle at the extent to which "merit" no longer seems to determine where people end up, to what degree will that arouse empathy for those *below* who are truly struggling and whose fates are shaped by similar degrees of luck or structural disadvantage? As it dawns on this elite class that people do not end up economically where they deserve to, the political implications may be striking.

"I've seen it in my research," says Doug Schoen, a pollster who has counseled Michael Bloomberg and Hillary Clinton, among others. "If you look at the lower part of the upper class, or the upper part of the upper middle class, there's a great deal of frustration. These are people who assumed that their hard work and conventional 'success' would leave them without worries over the quality of their lives. It's opening their eyes to things that are wrong with the economy more broadly. It's the type of rumbling that could lead to political volatility."

As we'll see a little later, this isn't the first time professionals have been gripped by this kind of status anxiety. The result of Lower Upper grumblings last time was known as the Progressive Era.

7

THE TYRANNY OF
DEAD IDEAS

It's time to step back and consider the big picture. We all know in our own lives how powerful the inertia of a Dead Idea can be, though often it's only in retrospect that we appreciate how hard it was to recognize, and break free of, its grip. People spend years in therapy examining reflexes formed in childhood that control their behavior decades later. Companies are often pushed to the brink of extinction before admitting that "the way we've always done things" no longer makes sense. The hunger for certainty and continuity in a changing world is part of being human. Even when it no longer serves our interests, we cling to what we think we know.

In our national life, as we've now seen, certain ideas that once seemed entirely plausible and useful have likewise become dangerous and counterproductive, closing our minds at precisely the moment in this global era when new ways of thinking are needed. Let's recap how these Dead Ideas tyrannize the American economic mind. The seminal change of our era—the news we most want to wish away—is that up to half the rising generation won't earn as much as their parents did. It's hard to think creatively about how to cope with this epochal development when we're in denial about it. Our blindness has been compounded by economists' successful campaign to persuade the American establishment that globalization and free trade are "good" for all of us, when both economic theory and common sense suggest that growing ranks of people are being hurt. The right response, as we've seen, isn't protectionism, but a new set of "protections" to assure that economic change is consistent with a decent society in a wealthy nation like the United States. This means that essentials like health care and pensions don't disappear with people's jobs, that adequate unemployment insurance is available, and so forth. There's no way to assure these arrangements without government's playing a bigger role, yet we're stuck thinking that employers should be our ultimate security blanket, not the state. It would be easy enough in theory to shift this responsibility toward government (and make business more competitive in the process), but that would require higher taxes, which we're wrongly convinced will hurt the economy.

Meanwhile, we know we'll never protect America's living standards over the longer term without improving our schools. Yet despite our system's chronic mediocrity, we cling to the conviction that America's unique fetish for local control and finance will get us out of the educational hole it has helped dig us into. At the same time, America's leadership class has believed that people basically end up, in economic terms, where they deserve to, so there's been little impetus to shake things up, despite the fact that larger economic forces now do more to shape people's fates.

Add it all up and today's outdated orthodoxy has us in a straitjacket. We can't admit what's happening due to globalization and rapid technological change, and couldn't do anything about it if we did. Our entire political and economic culture remains trapped in obsolete ways of thinking, leaving public discussion of these questions surreally disconnected from reality. Like your sister who can't see that her deadbeat husband is really no good for her, or Wall Street firms convinced that housing prices can only go up, the powers that be across American society can't see past the blinders that have been erected in their brains. From news professionals who rarely ask presidential candidates about schools because they're a "local" matter, to labor leaders who helped sink California governor Arnold Schwarzenegger's universal health care plan in 2008 because business wasn't picking up more of the cost, there's plenty of confusion to catalogue.

MONOPOLY DOWN, INEQUALITY UP

If today's Tyranny of Dead Ideas leaves business executives, professionals, policy makers, media observers, and other opinion leaders in a muddle, breaking free of it will force us to face up to two pivotal economic trends. The first is the end of an extraordinary era of U.S. dominance in the global economy. The second is the emergence of inequality as the preeminent economic issue of the twenty-first century.

Take the loss of American dominance first. As we've seen, after World War II, America's status as the only economy left standing kicked off an era of unprecedented industrial supremacy. "You had a sixty-year period where every new industry of huge value-added or breakthrough innovation or high risk—whether it was pharma, biotech, software, personal computing, or semiconductors—were all totally U.S.-based," said Bill Gates in 2007. This unrivaled position fueled habits of mind that no longer serve us well in an era when economic activity and power are becoming broadly distributed across the globe. The adjustment we face as a nation is very similar to that faced by businesses that have long had dominant market positions but which suddenly face real competition, thanks to regulatory or technological change or to the emergence of new market entrants. Firms operating in this situation have typically been fat and happy; the sudden exposure to competition exposes myriad inefficiencies if not downright craziness in "the way things have always been done." A period of painful rethinking and change ensues if the firm is to survive and thrive in its new environment. Often the managers who ran the business in the "good old days" can't make the transition; fresh blood is needed to bring the organization into the future. For the entire U.S. economy today, the need, and the psychological adjustment this entails, is the same.

When the American economy was dominant, after all, the old thinking sufficed. The kids *were* earning more than we had; we celebrated this fact en route to creating the highest consuming middle class the world had ever seen. Those who were hurt by the open trading regime we championed found new opportunities more readily available, because overall growth was so strong, and because advanced skills were not then a prerequisite for middle-class jobs. In that less competitive time (when health costs were also much lower), U.S. companies *could* subsidize much of our welfare state. This in turn let us luxuriate in naive attitudes toward taxes and the role of government, since companies themselves took on this quasi-government role. Few folks fell through the cracks, because the pattern then, unlike today, was lifetime employment by a single male breadwinner. America's dominant position also meant it wasn't urgent to raise all Americans to a higher level of skill and education; people earned decent livings without it. Finally, the existence of economic meritocracy, at least to our leadership class, seemed real enough. Barriers based on race and sex were falling, elite college admissions were becoming more inclusive, and the extreme earnings now common at the very top simply weren't the cultural norm. As Peter G. Peterson, the cofounder of the Blackstone Group, once remarked to me, Reginald Jones, who ran General Electric from 1972 to 1981, "was not a very wealthy man."

The erosion of America's commanding position in the world economy has meant the end of all this. But we have yet to adjust our outlook and behavior to the world we now occupy.

At the same time, inequality has emerged as the central economic issue of the twenty-first century. In the twentieth century, *stabilization* was the first major economic challenge—how to avoid the periodic meltdowns, epitomized by the Great Depression, that were so damaging. The second major challenge was *growth*—how to design policies that would best spur productivity and living standards. Between advances in central banking and macroeconomic management techniques on the one hand, and new insights into the way technology, market incentives, and investment drive growth on the other, real advances were made on both fronts. This doesn't mean the "end of history" has been reached on either topic (as the struggle to manage the credit crisis of 2008 made plain). But this progress allowed capitalism to create unprecedented increases in human welfare, improvements it is poised to spread more broadly around the world in the decades ahead.

Due to successes on these earlier challenges, the issue of inequality has now moved front and center. Partly this is because of the way mass media allow everyone on the planet to see how everyone else on the planet lives. Gross disparities in living standards are now both a spur for those who hope to grow rich as well as an affront to common notions of justice. Can it really be just for a relatively small group of people in the West to live in a consumer paradise, while literally billions of people elsewhere struggle without potable drinking water, flush toilets, and basic health and sanitation services? Questions of justice aside, will such disparities spark an eventual uprising?

Inequality *between* nations has actually been falling as growth takes off in less developed countries like China and India, which have learned to combine market incentives and technological "catch-up" to boost exports. *Within* nations, however, the gap between the top and bottom is widening. This is because technological change increases wages most rapidly for those with the most education. The benefits of growth thus accrue disproportionately to the most fortunate members of society, and to their well-schooled children. "Unless governments can ensure that educational attainment throughout the population rises fast enough to keep up with technological change," explains the economist Paul Romer, "faster worldwide growth in this century will be accompanied by growing inequality within each nation."

Managing the moral and political tensions associated with economic inequality is truly a global challenge. Not long ago, I asked a leading Chinese think tank analyst which of China's problems worried him most: the tottering banking system, the absence of pensions, the environmental degradation, or perhaps the decrepit health care system. Serious as these challenges were, he said, they wouldn't top his list. What worried him most was inequality: in particular, the prospect that simmering resentment in China's poor rural west over the wealth accumulating in China's eastern coastal cities would lead the government to "overreact" and launch redistribution schemes that would undermine China's remarkable growth. Remember, this was a member of the Communist Party talking! When communists are fretting about the effect of redistribution on growth, you know we're in a different world.

America's showdown with its Dead Ideas takes place in this broader global context. Indeed, people outside the United States would be happy to add a few other Dead Ideas to our list. The 5.6 billion people who don't live in the West deeply resent the presumption that 900 million westerners should be calling the global shots politically and economically. They'd also argue that the stunning gap between rich and poor nations is hurtling the system toward some kind of reckoning. A project called "The Miniature Earth" (at www.miniature-earth.com) captures the situation dramatically, through a presentation that asks us to imagine the world as a community made up of one hundred people. In such a world:

- 61 people are Asian, 12 are European, and 8 North American
- 43 people live without basic sanitation
- 18 live without an improved water source
- 6 people own 59 percent of the entire wealth of the community
- 13 are hungry or malnourished
- 14 can't read
- Only 7 are educated at a secondary level
- Only 12 have a computer
- Only 3 have an Internet connection
- If you keep your food in a refrigerator and your clothes in a closet, sleep in a bed, and have a roof over your head, you are one of the richest 25 people
- 53 people struggle to live on 2 dollars a day or less

Seen in this light, the stakes couldn't be higher, because the way the United States meets its current challenges will help shape the fate of the planet. What steps will America take to deal with growing inequality inside our borders? If we do too little, do we risk a protectionist backlash that will shut down markets to which poor countries need access if they're to rise? How do we keep a lid on the developing world's resentment in the meantime? Making workers in wealthy nations feel more secure without undermining the economic progress of the developing world will be the central balancing act to manage as our Dead Ideas head toward the cemetery.

Today's Dead Ideas didn't establish their tyranny on the strength of logic alone. They won't relinquish it by bowing to sweet reason either. As we've seen, various interests cling to Dead Ideas like barnacles, determined to extend their influence. Roughly 95,000 school board members stand ready to threaten the careers of those who would challenge our tradition of local school finance and governance. Top human resources executives at major companies, preferring to retain their benefits empires, advise their busy bosses not to let government mess with the corporation's role in providing social services. Certain tycoons will always want us to believe that higher taxes of any kind will strangle the economy, and they'll fund sophisticated propaganda to press their point. These interests will naturally be an obstacle to transcending the Tyranny of Dead Ideas. But in an era of unprecedented economic transformation, their sway has limits. Experts say we're likely to live through more change in the next thirty years than in the previous three hundred; in this extraordinary moment, the bigger impediment to our collective coping is our imagination. Once our thinking catches up to what's changing around us, people and institutions that seem to be obstacles will yield with surprising speed. Keynes had it right: "I am sure that the power of vested interests is vastly exaggerated," he wrote, "compared to the gradual encroachment of ideas."

It is to these destined ideas that we now turn.

PART TWO

TOMORROW'S DESTINED IDEAS

In 1928, if you had asked people whether the federal government should take aggressive steps to fight economic downturns, or to help senior citizens live decently in old age, or to ease the pain until jobless Americans could get back on their feet, most would have said no. "Rugged individualism" was the ethic of the age. By 1940, however, these propositions were considered common sense. The climate of opinion had been transformed by events. My argument is that a number of ideas that seem unthinkable or beyond the pale in 2009 will likewise seem completely mainstream and sensible by the year 2020. Let me be clear: I'm not predicting that it will take a calamity on the scale of the Great Depression for these changes to unfold. But the continued march of globalization and rapid technological change will have the same revolutionary effect on the way Americans think. Welcome, then, to a preview of tomorrow's "destined ideas"—ideas that are off-limits today but which are certain to reshape business and political life in the coming years.

TOMORROW'S DESTINED IDEAS

- Only government can save business
- Only business can save liberalism
- Only higher taxes can save the economy (and the planet)
- Only the (lower) upper class can save us from inequality
- Only better living can save sagging paychecks
- Only a dose of "nationalization" can save local schools
- Only lessons from abroad can save American ideals

In this part of the book we'll tease out these new ways of thinking and show how their ascent will force important groups to confront painful truths even as they help us move past our Dead Ideas. Business, for example, instinctively loathes the idea that it needs government to step up; but it does. Liberals are appalled by the thought that a just society can be achieved only with business's decisive contribution; but it's true. Ordinary Americans recoil from the notion that they may earn less but live as happily; yet they can. Until we open our minds to such new outlooks and dispositions, we'll remain trapped in a world of economic delusions.

As we proceed we won't be discussing every nitty-gritty detail; the fine print can come later. My aim is to sketch the big new ways of thinking that lie ahead. It's also important to note that I'm not trying to *persuade* you that these approaches represent the course we *should* take. I'm arguing that this is basically what's in the cards, that these new habits of mind are going to come to prevail as our Dead Ideas give way under the pressure of events. Our task is to get ready for the world that is being born. Our expectations and assumptions about everyday life are about to evolve, and this will reshape how we relate to our families, our workplaces, and our government. An updated version of American capitalism is about to emerge that can retain broad public support by combining growth and justice in ways suited to this moment in history. When we look back around the year 2020, we'll wonder why it didn't seem obvious that this was the way history was headed.

8

ONLY GOVERNMENT
CAN SAVE BUSINESS

The broad cry for a federal rescue of financial institutions in the fall of 2008 laid to rest the idea that Financial Markets Can Regulate Themselves. Most businesspeople assume this intervention will be an isolated episode, after which we'll return to the "normal" division of labor between the private and public sectors. But the truth is it's only the beginning. Long after the current crisis has passed, there will remain a deeper sense in which only government can save business in the years ahead, a development that will transform our conception of the proper role of each sector in our economy.

As we have seen in our review of the Dead Ideas tyrannizing America, soaring health care and pension burdens have become an unsustainable drag on business competitiveness. And the worst is yet to come, with experts forecasting that national health care costs alone will surge from 16 percent of GDP today to 20 percent by 2015. Yet a simple corporate abandonment of these costs isn't the answer, since it will leave millions of people vulnerable. The more corporations pursue this path, the greater will be the toll on the reputation of big business, which is already suffering because people think corporate America cares for little but its own profits.

Are the critics right? Consider the following scene, which is becoming a ritual at Fortune 500 board meetings across America. The CEO passes out a chart that shows the progress his team has made in getting a handle on health care and pension costs. The "before" line shows continued double-digit annual increases in the years ahead, devouring profits. The "after" line, sharply lower, shows the impact of a range of steps the company has taken, within the law, to reduce existing obligations. The board members, seated around a polished woodgrain conference table, agree it is impressive. A financial threat to shareholders has been contained. Combined with the relocation of many of the company's plants to less costly sites abroad, the outlook is much improved. A chorus of congratulations greets the CEO. Then, on rare occasions, a board member adds a thought. "I hope we're cognizant of the fact that this represents real hardship and leaves these people very exposed," he might say. "I hope we won't be taking positions outside the company that would prevent these people from getting some help." No one says a word. After an uncomfortable moment, the meeting moves on. Meanwhile, the company continues to lobby via its Washington trade association for lower overall taxes, making it impossible for government to extend its safety net as companies like this one withdraw their own.

Let's freeze that picture during the uncomfortable silence right after the concerned board member made his point. Critics would say this silence is a sign of malice, or at least damnable indifference to the fate of families being thrown to the wind. I know from my experience with business leaders that this isn't true. If we dig deeper, what we find instead is the confusion of decent people caught in a conflict between their duty to shareholders and their broader sympathies as human beings, without a new way of think-ing that would let them bridge the gap.

Consider the internal monologue of a typical CEO on these matters today. "We can't bear this social welfare burden any longer," he reckons. "These costs are killing us. And it doesn't feel as if it should be our responsibility. But we can't ask government to do more—they'd only make an even bigger mess, and besides, that would put us on the road to socialism. Plus they'd have to raise taxes, and that would kill the economy. And the left would slam us for dumping it all on someone else anyway. Let's ask our Republi-can friends what to do."

Enter the Republicans (the party of most business leaders today), who are happy to supply some suggestions. Let's keep lis-tening:

"Okay," the CEO's internal voice continues, "the Republicans say that bringing more market forces into health care will lower costs. Costs keep spiraling because people don't have enough 'skin in the game.' If we switch to high deductible, 'consumer directed' health care plans, they say, employees will be empowered to make better choices, and with their own money at risk they'll have a real stake in bringing costs down . . . What's that you say? Eighty per-cent of health care costs come from things like heart attacks or chronic diseases that are incurred above anyone's deductible, so this can't be the answer on costs? You say we'd be cynically 'empowering' employees to pay more for less coverage—and truly hurting folks who get sick? Well, it's hard to think that some mar-ket pressures in this crazy system wouldn't help. We ought to at least try it. Besides, what else do you want us to do? We can't sup-port some Democratic government takeover of health care. It's just wrong. What's more, the Republicans would screw us for breaking ranks, and we need them on free trade. At least these con-sumer directed plans will get some of these costs off the business.

And if everyone's moving in that direction we can't be singled out for criticism."

INSIDE THE BOX

You see the box the CEO is in. Put yourself in his shoes. The old answers don't add up, but it's hard to see fresh solutions through the fog of the capitalist mind. You're too busy running your firm under intense new global pressures to step back, connect the dots, and rethink matters not directly related to immediate business needs. The only way you can square the circle and psychologically escape from this dilemma—that is, lower business costs without increasing government's role, without raising taxes, without running afoul of Republican ideology, and (equally important) without feeling bad about yourself—is to shift more costs to workers, while simultaneously convincing yourself that you have to do this for the good of the company and the country, because this is what the system needs. Someone's got to make the tough choices. You subconsciously tune out reports that many workers are hurt by this, and if some news gets through to this effect, you tell yourself that if there's an issue here, it's for society to deal with somehow. It's bigger than any one company. Though you don't want government getting more involved. Well, anyway . . .

And so the circular rationalizations continue. And costs get shifted to workers, many of whom cannot afford to bear them; and bankruptcies soar among people who get sick; and hospital finances deteriorate as the ranks of the underinsured become a problem rivaling that of the uninsured. Seen this way, the CEO's inability to transcend the Tyranny of Dead Ideas leads to attitudes and behaviors that not only unintentionally inflict pain on others, but in the end boomerang and hurt his reputation. Because at the same time he is forcing squeezed workers to bear more costs, he's lining up board support for an enormous pay package for himself—seeing no link between the two, and believing, as the American economic mind does, that life's economic rewards generally flow according to merit. Later he wonders why big business and CEOs have such low standing in public opinion surveys. This drop in business's stature in turn hurts the cause of broader health care reform, because the business community is so powerful that it has to be at the heart of any coalition for change. Now business stands discredited, so prospects for reform grow dim. It's a depressing cycle.

The inevitable answer, though it cuts against the traditional corporate way of thinking, will be for government to pick up more of the social welfare burden, as it does in every other wealthy nation. When I say "only government can save business" in the long term, therefore, I'm not talking about Wall Street–style bailouts (although that has proved true enough). Instead, I mean salvation in two ways: both from the crippling costs of the central and antiquated role that business plays in America's welfare state, and from the reputational hit business will continue to suffer if it keeps nibbling away at the problem by shifting costs to workers or shrugging off these costs altogether.

As pragmatic businesspeople think this through, they'll see that there is no practical alternative. Asking individuals to bear the full cost of their health, pension, and related protections won't work, because in such an "every man for himself" system, sicker and poorer people get the shaft. Insurance schemes in decent societies by definition involve cross-subsidies and redistribution that can be handled only within larger groups. When it comes to government stepping up, the usual caricature—that a bigger role for Uncle Sam invariably means socialism—will finally lose its bite, because it's false. That line is generally taken by Republican partisans who fear that any expansion of government's role helps the Democrats and hurts them. Once upon a time this may have been the case, as when the Republican operative Bill Kristol urged his party in 1993 and 1994 to oppose anything that could be conceived of as a health

care "victory" for President Clinton. But this brand of obstruction-
ism, while entirely rational as a political matter for Republicans at
the time, simply can't deliver what American business needs in this
era to solve its problems. Farsighted Republicans know as much;
they're just not sure yet how to put a Republican stamp on the destined changes ahead.

To midwife the coming transformation, corporate America's
way of thinking will change. Executives will come to see government not as some alien foe but as a partner freeing them to meet
today's challenges without the burden of yesterday's unsustainable
social obligations. It's not as if business objects on principle to government's coming to the rescue, as we learned with the federal
government's extraordinary interventions during the market turmoil
after the subprime mortgage meltdown in 2008. Indeed, there's
something deeply hypocritical about devotees of free markets who
profess to adore laissez-faire outcomes 364 days a year, except on
the day when they run to the government to save them from their
disastrous bets. When it comes to health care and retirement, of
course, government won't be "bailing out" business as business; it
will merely, with business's support, be reclaiming social welfare
functions that ought to have been the government's responsibility
in the first place. The pressure of events in the years ahead will
force this overdue clarification of the private and public sectors'
proper roles in a modern economy. Business leaders have some
psychological distance to travel to get comfortable with these
arrangements, but the numbers—and the logic of the situation—
will prove irresistible.

CEOs have always been mostly Republican, and with good reason: calls for freer markets, lower taxes, and less regulation won the
natural sympathies of business leaders, especially in the decades
after World War II when capitalism was in a showdown with communism. But now, with communism dead, and with globalization

the main economic challenge, business leaders simply have not processed that a shift has occurred in what business needs from politics. Business desperately needs to rethink its social welfare role: whether a company offers its workers "too much" or "too little," it's nothing but a headache. As we've seen, moreover, merely shedding these costs isn't enough. Listen to the financier Wilbur Ross, who made billions when steel hit the skids and stands to make his next billion off the restructuring (via massive wage and benefit cuts) of the auto and auto parts industries: "I really do worry," he says, "and hope some semblance of the American standard of living can be saved for these folks." When even the vultures have qualms, you know change is in the wind.

To do right by their firms, and by public opinion, business leaders will have no choice but to scrap their reflexive allegiance to a misguided antigovernment creed. Even better, they'll help change it. Their need to get Uncle Sam to take on more of the benefits burden will run smack into the nihilistic "big government" rhetoric that has long dominated Republican thinking. In the years ahead, however, if Republican politicians want to help CEOs solve their biggest problems, this caricature of a political philosophy will have to give way to something more constructive. Just as the "Nixon to China" theory of history counsels that it will ultimately take a Democratic president to fix Social Security, it may likewise take a Republican president to bless the socialization of health and pension spending we need. It will take time to get there, vigilance to make sure more federal cash doesn't mean the dread "government-run health care," and probably golden parachutes for the phalanx of human resources executives whose benefits empires this vision threatens. Yet when the dust clears we'll still be far more of a low tax economy than Sweden or France. It would also hardly be the first time American business has learned to accommodate a new role for government in order to prosper. "What I have advocated is not wild radicalism," said Theodore Roosevelt of his trust-busting and regulatory initiatives a century ago. "It is the highest and wisest kind of conservatism."

THE END OF CAPITALISM AS WE KNOW IT

I can hear the groans already from the executive suite: "First the Wall Street bailout—now this? This is going to mean the end of capitalism as we know it." That's exactly right, but the point is, that's not a bad thing. My message is simple: Relax. It's going to be fine. Really.

The key to making this transition successful is to have government ramp up its role in health care and pensions in economically rational ways that don't bring the downsides that conservatives often fear. This is entirely doable. There's even a model right in front of us that people across the spectrum endorse: the mortgage interest deduction. Uncle Sam promotes home ownership with this subsidy without telling people what kind of house they need to buy, how many rooms they need to have, where the closets should be located, et cetera. This kind of voucher approach to services— through which government makes subsidies available to those who need them, and helps set up the market so it works fairly and meets public goals—can apply in many terrains. The federal government could find a way to implement stronger health care and pension protections that would be different from the approach taken by much of Europe. How might that work?

Take health care first. Britain, Canada, and a number of European nations feature government-run "single payer" systems in which private insurers have no role and most doctors are employees of the state. These systems deliver universal coverage, but also impose what most Americans would feel are intolerable waiting times for common services; they also depend to a great extent on medical innovation coming from the United States in areas from drugs to medical devices to advanced procedures. But rather than follow this path, America could achieve universal coverage while still preserving the benefits of market forces by in effect giving every American—regardless of preexisting conditions—a voucher with which to buy an adequate group health plan from among competing private insurers. If wealthier Americans wanted to spend more money and get additional services or protections beyond what the government voucher covered, they could. The health insurance industry would be reformed to look more like a regulated utility, ending the perverse dynamic under which insurers maximize profits by competing to cover people who are in relatively good health and shunning those who aren't. Yet we'd retain the positive value that large health payers can bring, chiefly the innovative use of systemwide data to drive changes in medical practice and delivery that can boost the efficiency and quality of care. The revamped system might be financed with contributions from government, individuals, and business, but with business contributing at permanently lower levels than the sector spends today. It could also be financed via a new dedicated tax (such as a VAT), getting business out of the equation entirely.

Something like this model—and there are any number of such proposals floating around—will get surprising traction once the capitalist mind opens. Business leaders will realize that it's essential in the twenty-first century for people to have access to group health coverage outside the employment context. The absence of a reliable way to do this today not only strands tens of millions of people who don't work, or who work part time, or who work for employers who do not offer such coverage; it's also a serious barrier to entrepreneurship, since people who want to strike out on their own often do not because it means putting their medical coverage at risk. (I know something about this, because my wife and I discovered a few years ago that we were uninsurable in the individual market, even though our doctors said we were perfectly healthy.)

In addition, achieving universal coverage along these lines is not inconsistent with introducing a greater consumer culture to health care. The trick in this regard is to make sure that poorer or sicker people aren't exposed to costs they can't bear. One possibility is to institute high deductible plans that would also limit a person's out-of-pocket expense every year to no more than some reasonable percentage of income; such plans are generally favored by conservatives, and if they are designed with such an income-related cap, this would address the justifiable worries of liberals. To be sure, such consumer directed health plans can never be the full answer for soaring national health costs, because 80 percent of health costs are incurred for major events, chronic diseases, and hospitalizations with price tags well above anyone's deductible. But bringing some consumer mentality even to 20 percent of national health care spending would introduce market forces to a whopping $400 billion annual market. It's hard to think there wouldn't be some positive ripple effect on the broader health care culture if enough of us routinely asked doctors (to cite one of countless such examples) why today's visit cost $300 instead of $150.

NEST EGGS NEEDED

For pensions, a similar approach and role for government (as opposed to business) is possible as well. Here we have a head start because government has long provided a basic benefit via Social Security. The problem is that millions of Americans save so little that they are still closing in on retirement without an adequate nest egg. Many lower income and even middle income Americans can't afford to save; they find it hard enough to make ends meet. One potential answer: new "universal 401(k)" plans could be established through which all citizens could save tax-free for retirement, with the federal government matching individual contributions progressively. Lower income folks who feel they can't afford to save today might be encouraged to save $500 or $600 a year because they would receive a two-to-one match until their account reached $2,000 each year. Middle income savers might get a one-to-one match; higher income savers might get fifty cents on the dollar. (Companies would be free to make contributions as well, but would not be required to.)

As these examples illustrate, in both health care and pensions, the idea is to pursue a new hybrid public-private approach through which government helps people meet the economic challenges of our time by harnessing market forces for public purposes, while funding the new arrangements in ways equal to the need. Meanwhile, the role of business is reduced over time, except where firms decide it is useful to offer supplements to these different vehicles in order to attract and retain employees.

Adequate unemployment insurance would also go far to save business from the backlash that accompanies a dynamic global economy in which jobs are no longer as secure. Today only a fraction of jobless Americans are eligible for unemployment insurance, and this typically replaces only 30 to 35 percent of salary for a maximum of six months. While we don't want an overly generous system that encourages idleness rather than the search for the next job, today's overly stingy system leaves too many working families in desperate straits when business conditions change.

Finally, in addition to progressively funded individual pension accounts, government could find ways to create more equal chances for people to acquire assets from birth. A number of "endowment" proposals, for example, would have government deposit $1,000 or more a year in accounts for all children during their first five years of life so that even children from poorer families could benefit from the miracle of compound interest. This is another way that creative approaches from government, with business support, might make it easier for people in a fast-changing economy to accumulate assets with which to tide themselves over during difficult times. This could free business to respond to rapidly changing circumstances without being exposed to social protests every time it finds it has to cut or move jobs.

In the end, something like this direction is our fate. And when government saves business in these ways, it will make perfect sense. If we're on the cusp of decades of wrenching challenges from places like China and India, doesn't American business have enough to do without assuring everybody's health care and pension security, too? What's more, getting corporations out of the business of social welfare doesn't mean American enterprise is "off the hook" when it comes to these big social challenges. In fact, business will be playing a vital and (some would say) surprising role.

9

ONLY BUSINESS
CAN SAVE LIBERALISM

If many conservatives will at first recoil from the idea that only government can save business in the era ahead, many on the left will resist the notion that only business can save liberalism. But for at least three major reasons, it's true.

Start with trade. Liberals often like to cast business as the enemy of social justice. And, to be sure, there will always be enough rotten firms run by greedy bastards to fill a rogue's gallery. But the more profound and unappreciated fact is that in a global economy, business is the great liberal hope—perhaps the only force that can stop the left in rich countries from hurting poor people everywhere else. This is a hard conversation to have honestly, because it explodes the conventional ideological categories. The left is supposed to care about the poor and disadvantaged; the right and big business are supposed to be venal and heartless. But on global trade these positions end up effectively reversed, because of tradeoffs many liberals pretend don't exist.

To see why, ask left-leaning trade critics how they think about their aspirations for the millions of people struggling to achieve a better life here in America in the context of a defensible moral stance toward the billions beyond our shores who seek the same betterment—some of whom want to move here, and most of whom want to trade with us in ways that may put American jobs or wages at risk. The stock answer from the left is that we should "lift the bottom" by raising wages and workplace standards overseas. Surely this is an important point. Abusive practices that leave U.S. workers competing against prison labor or child labor aren't right. But there's a further point that most liberals won't acknowledge: even if their ideal reforms were instituted, many foreign workplaces would still feature lower costs that American workers can't match. If you're a union leader or an American politician whose con-stituents are affected by this competitive threat, your resulting pro-tectionist bias is understandable. But Americans not directly affected can ask a different question: Why is it "liberal" to deny poor workers abroad the chance to rise by virtue of their one competitive advantage? It only takes a little thinking along these lines to realize that in a broader global view, business may ultimately be a more "progressive" force than American labor or government in the decades ahead. That's because big business is generally the most powerful group fighting for the reciprocal free trade and access to markets on which poor countries' ability to rise depends.

The contours of this reality are almost never explored, because it cuts against the standard "liberals care about poor people, busi-ness doesn't" paradigm that skews media coverage. One rare and fascinating exception, which received little notice at the time, was a long conversation the liberal globalization critic William Greider conducted with former Treasury secretary Robert Rubin, then a member of Citigroup's top management team, in July 2006 in *The Nation*. Greider pressed Rubin on his fears that globalization was causing a convergence of wages between richer nations like the United States and poorer developing countries.

"The question is," Rubin said, "will convergence happen because their wages go up or because our wages go down?"

"That leads right to my next question," Greider said, querying Rubin from what he described as the camp of "reasonable, intelligent, and rational" left-leaning critics. From this point of view, Greider explained, the global trading system needs some mechanism that requires developing countries to build a rising wage standard into their economy. Perhaps it would be a minimum wage set relative to their level of prosperity. "Because the world is huge and full of poor people and producers," he went on, "multinationals can constantly . . . move their production to the next cheaper country. Labor would say: If you are not going to stop the process of convergence, you are at least going to moderate it. Because you've forced rising wages at the bottom, you have some chance of not completely decimating high-wage, blue-collar labor in America and elsewhere."

"Well, I guess there are two pieces to that," Rubin replied. If Greider was saying that we should strive to improve the distribution of income in poor countries, because this would be good for everybody concerned, Rubin was happy to sign on. But he suspected that many people who made Greider's argument were really trying to close down imports of lower priced goods from poorer nations altogether. "It is a complicated question," Rubin added. "The one hope that some of these countries have to take their people out of abject poverty is that their labor-cost advantage will result in a shift in production to their countries from the place that it's now taking place, and if you require them to not take advantage of their labor-cost advantage, then you really have condemned them to poverty."

Greider replied that what we're seeing now is a race to the

bottom, as multinationals keep shifting production to the next cheap country they find. Work gets shifted from Thailand to Sri Lanka, for example, once Thai workers start to organize and demand higher wages. "Yeah," said Rubin, "but what makes it complicated is that it may be the only way for the people in Sri Lanka to get out of abject poverty. . . . Would you say the people of Sri Lanka have to stay in abject poverty to prevent that from happening?" Both men finally reached a tentative agreement that the right objective for the global system is that production take place everywhere, but that poor countries develop institutions that allow workers to share in the economic gains their country is experiencing.

Greider is one of America's most thoughtful and passionate advocates of a fairer shake for labor, and a prescient voice on the impact of globalization. Yet what's fascinating in this dialogue is that it is repeatedly Rubin, the voice of big business, who defends the right of the poorest people in the world to climb out of poverty in the only practical way available to them. Who's the "progressive" in this exchange? As Rubin says, it's complicated. The reality, of course, is that big business won't be helping the world's poor out of the goodness of its heart; executives obviously have no fiduciary duty to lift the bottom. But so what? Merely by acting on what some critics deride as the corporation's "psychopathic" drive for lower costs and higher profits, business will end up doing a good measure of the Lord's work.

Business leaders need to recognize that the social contribution corporations make by lifting the world's poor in this way will be as vital as anything they do by "going green." Only business will push consistently for the open markets that will let poor countries rise, because the American left is constrained by the threat to its constituents. As we've seen, although the left is correct to worry that globalization isn't good for millions of Americans, the answer is not protectionism, but better "protections" (in areas like health care, pensions, and unemployment insurance) and new efforts to make sure non-offshorable jobs offer a path to the middle class. By pressing to keep markets open, and by transferring technological and managerial know-how from rich to poor nations and their citizens, global business—yes, those dread multinationals—will be the unlikely champion of the world's poor.

LIBERALISM AND EFFICIENCY:
TOGETHER AT LAST

The second and perhaps similarly unexpected sense in which business is poised to save liberalism is via its drive for efficiency. As we've discussed, two of the most inefficient sectors of our economy are health care and education, where America spends far more than other advanced nations with far less to show for it. Making these sectors run smarter and better will become a national imperative in the era of permanent fiscal pressure ahead, an effort with special stakes for liberals who believe in using government for affirmative purposes. Even if taxes are inevitably going up, there will be limits to how high American voters will let taxes rise, and that means the vast waste in our health care and education systems will soon take a huge bite out of other liberal priorities. Put simply, every dollar that goes to Medicare that isn't needed for quality health care is a dollar that liberals can't spend on a poor child. That's what the tradeoffs will look like before long. And whether the left likes it or not, business is the one social force that can help solve this dilemma through efficiency-boosting innovations that deliver more for less.

I'm not talking about the far right's pure privatization agenda, which aims to privatize profit in these sectors while socializing risk. (The best example is the individual market for health insurance, where "success" means selling coverage to everyone except people who might actually need it.) And it's impossible to predict the precise forms business innovation will take in these areas. But some examples can give a feel for what's in store. Minute Clinics is the nation's largest provider of retail health care in the United States, with more than five hundred clinics now located inside big stores across the country. People can see nurse practitioners there seven days a week (no appointment required) for such common issues as ear infections, strep throat, minor burns, wart removal, pregnancy testing, and various vaccines. Typical visits last ten to fifteen minutes. The cost for most of these treatments is $49 to $69, far less than the price in a traditional doctor's office, and most insurance is accepted. Unsurprisingly, Minute Clinics has been opposed by some local doctors, who see the upstart retailer cutting into their revenue. But by emphasizing to patients the importance of having a primary care doctor for ongoing care, and by referring them to local doctors for follow-up, the chain has diffused resistance and positioned itself as the kind of convenient, low-cost, high-tech health provider that was previously unheard of in America. So far, the company's 2 million patient visits and 99 percent customer satisfaction rating suggest it is indeed possible to build a better mousetrap here.

Or take the for-profit Edison Schools, which, despite its tumultuous history, deserves credit for researching ways to revolutionize the traditional school model via "$100,000 teachers." Their nascent effort is a classic case of necessity being the mother of invention; in this instance, the desperate shortage of good teachers in poor neighborhoods is inspiring a creative response. Edison is convinced that much higher salaries will be needed to draw the teaching talent these children need to the classroom, but it also believes that fiscally strapped school districts would never swallow the tax hike such pay increases would entail if they were required across a teacher corps of today's size. Thus their idea: find a way to use half as many teachers in a school as is typical today, but pay them twice as much. It's the kind of big idea that public schools could never pursue because of a web of existing union rules and regulations, not to mention the system's incremental mind-set. The idea is to make this new teacher staffing model effective by reengineering the way schools do their work. Students, especially at the middle and high school level, would spend more time each day working alone or in small groups with the help of improved educational software; at other times, older students would tutor younger students as well. If done right, Edison believes the new model holds the promise of boosting achievement, student development, and teacher satisfaction. The greater freedom private firms like Edison have to experiment with such approaches could point the way toward a broader rethinking of the teaching profession, and eventually help public schools reorganize themselves to be more efficient and effective.

Finally, consider higher education. Making college affordable is a vital liberal goal; it's the path to economic opportunity for those born with little, and essential for well-informed democratic citizenship. But the traditional liberal means for pursuing this goal—offering grants and increasing volumes of student loans—often has the perverse effect of enabling colleges to raise tuitions ever higher. The only sustainable answer is to reengineer the cost structure and value delivered by the sector as a whole.

Business will be critical in this endeavor, because as higher education is currently structured, so many laws of economics seem not to apply. In most industries, for example, competition reduces costs; in higher education, it sparks an "arms race" of amenities that raise costs. Schools vie for the best students and research faculty to win better rankings, which raises prestige, which draws better students, which boosts alumni giving, which funds new labs, which draws new top faculty, and so on. In the war for top talent, schools rush to build fancier dormitories, glitzier student unions, Nobel-ready labs, Olympics-quality gyms, and Broadway-style theaters. Families now expect these amenities, college presidents moan, and no single school can stint on them lest they lose applicants to the competition. "If everyone agreed to cut physical plant and amenities by half, could we still provide the same education?" asks Gordon Winston, an economist at Williams College. "I think the answer is yes."

The federal government has unintentionally fueled the scholastic "arms race" by vastly expanding access to student loans—on the one hand, giving kids their shot at a degree; on the other, facilitating tuition hikes that would otherwise prove unsustainable. At the same time, the rise in private tuitions has made it easier for states to ratchet up public tuitions as well, hurting the bulk of the nation's students. What we're left with is a higher education establishment that now consumes more than $350 billion each year, in part delivering a good education, and in part relying on an explosion in student indebtedness to bankroll facilities and faculty research having little to do with undergraduate learning. To be sure, some state schools and troubled private colleges have become leaner. Nevertheless, says Charles Clotfelter, an economist at Duke University, "higher education is the biggest service industry that hasn't gone through substantial, gut-wrenching restructuring."

What might such restructuring entail? Online degree-granting firms like the University of Phoenix are challenging the current high-cost model with computer-based offerings tailored to adult students hungry for professional advancement. Their customized programs are breaking new ground in teaching and learning, and their lower infrastructure costs offer a new model for keeping tuition affordable. To be sure, it is early days yet, and the threat from such low-cost innovators will never threaten Harvard and Yale. But millions of students each year go deeply into debt to matriculate at thousands of American institutions outside those top few hundred with name brands, and substitutes will exist before long that offer equal or superior educations for less. As new firms emerge that better measure and publicize comparisons of the quality of education that different colleges deliver, a consumer culture will finally gain a foothold in higher education, pressuring the sector to adopt more cost-effective approaches across the board. Business will be central to these developments.

Harnessing competition, technology, and transparency in such ways to squeeze more out of every dollar is essential if we're to extend better health care and schooling to the millions now left behind, while also limiting the tax increases required as America ages. Only business has the innovative energy to help force change here with the scale and speed that liberal goals require.

CITIZEN CEO

The final sense in which business is poised to save liberalism is as a *constituency for the common good.* In my experience, executives have a huge blind spot when it comes to their potential role in the broader public debate. That's because firms have viewed their advocacy mostly through the prism of self-interested lobbying. There's a reason: a company's return on political investments—say, for an obscure tax break or federal contract—is astronomically higher than any real business investment it can make. This isn't well understood. Recall that when it comes to ordinary investment decisions, companies calculate their cost of capital and pursue the most attractive projects exceeding that "hurdle rate." Twelve percent per year is a rough estimate of the cost of capital for U.S. firms. In lobbying, a 12 percent return is often realized *every few hours.*

The mortgage giant Fannie Mae, for example, used to spend around $9 million a year lobbying to preserve federal guarantees that lowered its financing costs; depending on whom you believe, this subsidy was worth at least $20 billion a year (and the cost to taxpayers ultimately ended up being far higher). The Pentagon may offer the most measurable examples. The defense contractor Lockheed Martin spent $55 million on lobbying between 1999 and 2006, during which time it won roughly $90 billion in (mostly no-bid) contracts. Boeing spent $57 million over the same period and was rewarded with about $81 billion in contracts.

Beyond this lucrative emphasis on lobbying for their own bottom line reasons, many senior businesspeople worry that they'd be wasting their time on bigger issues because "nothing ever happens" in Washington—at least not at the pace they're used to when it comes to producing results in their companies. Finally, there's the fear factor. When Starbucks CEO Howard Schultz tried to get other corporate leaders to join him in 2005 to appear on a special television program on CNBC calling attention to the health care crisis, he was barely able to pull it off. "It wasn't easy to get CEOs to appear publicly on this issue," he told me. One CEO even withdrew after agreeing to join, telling Schultz, "I just can't be out front on this." "It's the cloud Hillary [Clinton] created when she tried to change the system" in 1993, Schultz says. "People burned her so badly and everyone remembers that. It's a subject people don't want to touch."

Yet this sentiment is changing fast. And many top CEOs are seeing they have the power to shape the debate. Lee Scott of Wal-Mart, for example, generated national headlines in 2006 merely by stating the obvious in a speech: that health care is a problem that business and government need to tackle together. In 2007, when Scott and longtime Wal-Mart critic Andrew Stern of the Service Employees International Union came together at the heart of a new coalition of business, labor, and public policy groups to fight for affordable health care for every American, it signaled a new era in which business would step forward even with the strangest of "strange bedfellows." (Readers should be aware that I have served as an adviser to Wal-Mart.) Several other such diverse coalitions have also emerged.

Bill Novelli, the head of AARP, believes that corporate America has reached the point of financial pain on health care where it is ready to act. "We've got to get corporations to really weigh in, to go to the White House and the Congress and say, 'The game is up, we can't take this anymore,'" he says. "I do believe there will be a groundswell—maybe even a corporate revolution."

As Novelli and others recognize, the challenges posed by the Tyranny of Dead Ideas are forcing business leaders to take this broader angle of vision. When corporate critics have assailed their firms in recent years, exasperated CEOs and top executives have complained privately. "What do they want from us?" they've said to me. "Our company can't solve the country's health care problem—or environmental problem, or wage problem, or pension problem, or you name your favorite major problem—by ourselves!" What I tell them, and what they're coming to realize, is that no one expects business leaders to solve these problems on their own. But critics do expect business leaders—and fairly, given their influence—to come out of their cocoons to help shape the public debate on how we tackle these challenges, and to support economically rational reforms that can make American capitalism work for everyone, not just the few. Once they get their feet wet in this unfamiliar terrain, CEOs will quickly come to appreciate that this is in business's enlightened self-interest. As this new way of thinking supplants business's traditional reluctance to step out publicly, and the "safety in numbers" dynamic takes hold, we'll see business leaders play a new and decisive role as a constituency for the broader public interest on a host of issues related to our Dead Ideas. As today's plethora of green corporate initiatives already under way suggests, once the slumbering giant is awakened, it can mobilize to deliver the goods.

The bottom line? A number of commonsense goals liberals have long pursued will finally get traction when business decides in the coming years to get behind them. Once business starts playing this farsighted role, it will have an easier time getting credit for its other social contributions that are often taken for granted—such things as innovation, investments in research and development, training employees, and promoting basic social virtues in the workplace, including punctuality, hard work, cooperation, and thrift.

10

ONLY HIGHER TAXES CAN SAVE THE ECONOMY (AND THE PLANET)

I believe we have a five to ten year window of opportunity to show our foreign lenders that we're going to be serious about this. Five to ten years, and it's closing. And I think it's closer to five than to ten. . . . Keep in mind, we're the largest debtor nation in the history of mankind, and it's getting worse, not better.

David Walker, U.S. comptroller general,
before the Senate Budget Committee, January 2008

Recall what we learned earlier. Higher taxes are inevitable, though you'd never know it from both political parties' aversion to discussing this fact. This isn't a disputable question. A few numbers remind us why. Today federal spending is about 20 percent of GDP. (That's down from 22 percent under Presidents Ronald Reagan and George H. W. Bush, by the way, so all the talk about George W. Bush having been a "big government conservative" was demonstrably a hoax.) At the same time, there is roughly $40 trillion in unfunded liabilities in our health care and pension programs, which we will need to pay for as the baby boomers move into their sixties. (And that's before you toss in trillions more in the unfunded health care and pension plans of state and local governments, another time bomb.) Unreformed, these surging programs are projected to take federal spending toward 30 percent of GDP by 2030. Federal taxes, meanwhile, are 18.8 percent of GDP today, down from nearly 21 percent at the end of the Clinton era. Serious people—by which I mean those willing to acknowledge that the number 30 is bigger than the number 18.8—know that this means our already record budget deficits are slated to soar to banana-republic-like heights, with calamitous economic consequences, unless spending is slowed, taxes raised, or both. On spending, to be sure, we need to slow the growth of our health care and pension programs, but enormous success might mean these programs push spending only to 25 percent of GDP instead of 30 percent, still vastly higher than today. And even if these trims in projected spending don't hurt vulnerable seniors (which they might), as a practical matter such restraint seems wildly improbable, given that even when "small government" Republicans dominated Washington a few years ago they balked at the idea of trimming a few teensy billions from the next trillion in planned Medicaid spending.

As a result, we're looking at one of two scenarios in the next decade. The first is "Deficits and Denial," under which we'll answer the question: "How long will foreign creditors like China tolerate our mad course and bankroll epic U.S. deficits before pulling the plug, sparking a dollar crisis that forces us to change our ways abruptly" (what the pros call a "hard landing")? The other scenario is "Grow Up and Pay Up," under which we decide short of such a crisis that we simply have to stop slipping the bill to our kids for tax cuts we choose to shower on the wealthy, wars we decide to fight, and general levels of government that we prefer not to pay for. Either way, and even with aggressive spending trims, taxes are going up. And here's the surprise: *in Washington, this is common knowledge!* Newt Gingrich has told me as much, as have senior House Republican leaders. So, as we saw earlier, did two of John McCain's top economic advisers. They'll tell *me,* but they won't tell you. Why? Because the tax issue is seen as so potent in elections that both Republicans and Democrats (for reasons of offense and defense respectively) feel they have to choose between full disclosure and winning. Put this way, candor doesn't stand a chance.

But the distant rumblings of reality can be heard. A few conservative thinkers are already lamenting that their movement's moment has passed because taxes will have to go up to pay for the boomers' retirement; the cause of smaller government, they wail, is now doomed! (This was always mathematically obvious to anyone who looked out more than a few years, which tells you all you need to know about the myopia of some conservative polemicists.)

Once this rendezvous with reality trickles down from conservative intellectuals to pols, and liberals find the courage to say the obvious, we'll start the debate we need: not about *whether* taxes *should* go up, but *given* that taxes *are* going up, what's the best way to fund the government we want, consistent with strong economic growth and other vital goals such as saving the planet? That's the new $3 trillion question (the rough amount Uncle Sam needs to raise each year to balance the budget), and, viewed properly, it's an enormous opportunity. A good way to think about it was suggested to me by Kevin Hassett of the American Enterprise Institute. Hassett dreams of a kind of Federal Reserve of Taxation—an unelected body (comprised of economists like himself, naturally) charged with making sure our tax system delivers the revenue we need while doing the least harm to the economy. If we had such an entity, Hassett told me, "then it's absolutely true that you could get your taxes-as-a-share-of-GDP level higher without affecting growth." It may be an economist's fantasy but it's also a useful framework. You politicians agree on how much money the system has to raise, it argues—then get out of the way and we'll devise a system that does this in the most economically desirable way possible. Economists I've talked to say the basic contours would be

agreed to by colleagues across the political spectrum. The system
that resulted would look very different from the one we have today.

CORPORATIONS ARE PEOPLE, TOO

Today we raise about 95 percent of federal revenue from income,
payroll, and corporate taxes—meaning that we basically tax work
and business activity, things you'd think we'd want to encourage.
Income taxes account for roughly half of all federal revenue today.
Payroll taxes account for about one-third; these are the dread FICA
deductions in your paycheck, along with related taxes, which in
theory are earmarked for Social Security and Medicare but in fact
are used for all government purposes. Corporate taxes account for
much of the rest. By contrast, excise or "sin" taxes—mostly on
alcohol, tobacco, and gasoline, substances whose use we presum-
ably want to discourage—represent only 3 percent of federal revenue, down from 9 percent forty years ago. (Customs duties, which
once represented the bulk of U.S. revenue, are now basically a
rounding error.)

Dig deeper and this revenue composition looks even more like
bad economics. Corporate taxes in the United States, for example, are
the second highest among developed countries. We raise 11.5 percent
of federal revenue from this source, while Europe raises 8 to 9 percent. Democrats often act as if these taxes are somehow a "free-
bie," paid by impersonal entities, not by real people. That conceit is
false. "Corporations" don't pay taxes, people do. These taxes are
ultimately borne by shareholders or employees. And corporate
taxes fundamentally affect where multinational firms decide to
locate, decisions that should be a major concern of policy makers
aiming to keep and attract good paying jobs in the United States.
High corporate taxes hurt American workers. It's that simple.

Today's payroll tax regime is likewise ill advised. The system
was introduced seven decades ago with a tax of just 2 percent on the

first $3,000 of wages; now the Social Security tax alone is 12.4 percent on roughly the first $106,000 earned, plus 2.9 percent of total wages for Medicare. At this point the payroll tax is not only regressive (taking a bigger bite out of lower income folks than from higher earners), but has grown so high in the aggregate that seven in ten families pay more in payroll taxes than in income taxes. Yet simply making payroll taxes more progressive raises problems of its own. Some suggest that a way to fix Social Security's financial deficit would be to eliminate the cap on the amount of earnings subjected to the 12.4 percent payroll tax, so that it would apply to a person's entire income. While at first blush this step might seem fair, if it were done in addition to proposals to return marginal income tax rates to the 39.6 percent that prevailed under President Clinton, it would effectively boost marginal rates beyond 50 percent—and this would be before high tax states and localities add what could be another 7 to 10 percent. You don't need to be a Reagan Republican to think that marginal income tax rates at these levels would have negative economic effects, especially when compared with other ways of raising the revenue we need. It's worth noting in this regard that while the United States raises about 35 percent of its total revenue (including state and local taxes) from the personal income tax, other Western countries as a whole raise just 25 percent from this source. (In Norway the figure is 22 percent; in Sweden, 32; Finland, 31; Italy, 25; Spain, 18; and Britain, 29.)

As we rethink our tax structure to prepare for the inevitable rise in overall taxes, the economically saner path is to tax work and business *less* while taxing consumption and carbon *more*. To be sure, modestly higher marginal income tax rates on the wealthiest citizens are also justified, since this group has reaped the benefit of virtually all of the economy's productivity gains over the last twenty years, gains that mostly came when structural changes in the economy (outside anyone's control) rewarded people who had skills suited to our high-tech age. In addition, we know that marginal rates at Clinton-era levels of 39.6 percent were consistent with robust economic growth. Yet the more general thrust in the coming era of tax reform should be to reduce (or eliminate) corporate income taxes and to reduce payroll taxes, while increasing consumption and energy taxes to plug the gap and then lift overall revenues as they become needed.

The leading candidate for a consumption tax is the so-called value added tax, or VAT, which is used by twenty-nine other advanced industrial countries. Why are we the great exception? The former Treasury secretary Lawrence Summers says that there is no enthusiasm for it because liberals view the VAT as regressive and conservatives see it as a huge money machine. We'll get a VAT, Summers quips, when liberals realize it is a huge money machine and conservatives realize it is regressive! The unrelenting fiscal pressures ahead will force precisely the change in outlook Summers describes. And liberals will find that they can offset the regressive tilt of a VAT in several ways: first, by using it to fund progressive programs (like universal health coverage); second, by using a fraction of the proceeds to boost subsidies to the working poor; or third, by exempting certain basic necessities from the tax.

Today consumption taxes at all levels in the United States account for only 8.5 percent of revenue, compared to 30 percent in other industrial nations. Remember: Europe's economic woes stem mostly from limits placed on the ability of firms to fire (and thus hire) people, and from rules preventing product market competition—policies the United States won't (and shouldn't) emulate. But many European and Scandinavian notions about tax structure are sound. A shift toward this smarter, growth-friendly brand of taxation is in our future.

RAISE TAXES, SAVE THE WORLD

So: we've seen that higher taxes will be needed before long to save the economy, in the sense of closing otherwise epic and untenable budget deficits, and to fund expansions of health care, pension, and related protections that ease worker anxiety, make business more competitive, and prevent a protectionist backlash. These unavoidable tax hikes will give us a chance to rethink the way we tax ourselves in order to best promote economic growth. But there are other things higher taxes can do for us—like save the planet!

Whether you're passionate about the threat of climate change or just concerned that the worst might be half true, virtually everyone agrees it's prudent to lower our emissions of carbon dioxide substantially. Despite all the hand wringing, however, virtually no progress has been made thus far in reducing emissions in proportion to the need. Meanwhile, the emerging consensus among business groups and politicians to implement some version of a "cap and trade" system regulating emissions in the United States will probably not get us where we need to go, either.

Why not? Under a "cap and trade" approach, government sets some allowable aggregate level of emissions, and then distributes the right to emit, either (ideally) by auctioning off permits, or by simply allocating them in some way. This may create windfalls for various insiders able to rig a giveaway to themselves. But beyond such potential scams, anyone familiar with the way regulated industries routinely capture and shape the actions of regulators knows there is a high probability that the overall level of carbon dioxide reductions will not be close to what environmental experts say is required, and that the limits will be relaxed over time. In addition, because there will be a market for emissions permits (that's the trade part of "cap and trade"), there are likely to be large and frequent fluctuations in the price firms must pay to emit carbon dioxide, at least if Europe's experience to date with such a system is any guide. This uncertainty is fatal for businesspeople who need to make long-term investments. If you're a utility executive trying to decide whether to invest in, say, expanding current coal capacity that may not come on line for a decade, or to move instead to renewable energy modes that cost much more now but might be cost effective depending on what the price of carbon emissions is down the road, this inability to predict your costs can be paralyzing.

Given these shortcomings, why is "cap and trade" emerging as the likely U.S. response? Because it lets politicians avoid enacting something that could be called a "tax" on carbon. Note that if carbon permits are auctioned off, emitters will still pass along the cost in the form of higher prices, so consumers won't really be off the hook; only politicians will be, which is the idea. And it is true that a "cap and trade" arrangement should create incentives for entrepreneurs to pursue new technologies that accelerate the progress we'll need to curb our reliance on dirty fuels. But the better economic path, if we're serious about carbon dioxide, is some form of explicit carbon tax that consistently and predictably raises the price of carbon-intensive products enough to reflect their real cost to society, and thus reduces their use. Lester Brown, the president of the Earth Policy Institute, says that if the full social costs of carbon-based energy were reflected in its price (including subsidies to oil companies, military spending to preserve access to Middle Eastern supplies, and the potential impact of climate change), a gallon of gasoline would cost more like $13, not the $4 that already generates cries of outrage. Filling up a twenty-gallon tank would cost $260. Even if this estimated gap were only half as big, we'd still be underpricing the true social cost of our oil addiction by four to five dollars a gallon. "Socialism collapsed because it did not allow the market to tell the economic truth," Brown says. "Capitalism may collapse because it does not allow the market to tell the ecological truth."

You don't have to be quite as apocalyptic as Brown to see that higher taxes can discourage the use of carbon-heavy forms of energy and create market incentives for investment in cleaner alternatives. Indeed, we had a preview of the power of these incentives in the summer of 2008, when the spike in gas prices past $4.00 led to an unprecedented surge in consumer purchases of compact, high mileage cars at the expense of gas-guzzling SUVs and trucks. Prices work. Higher taxes are therefore the key to jump-starting the "green economy" that politicians claim to covet but which only markets with proper price signals can call into existence.

Will our "leaders" ever talk honestly about our tax future, and treat us like adults? Or are we doomed to collective lying until both parties raise taxes anyway? Given the depressing imperatives of American politics, we're probably looking at the latter scenario, but it's better if the rest of us can read the tax hike on the wall and start shaping the debate about how best to raise taxes in ways that help the economy. Foreigners regard our conspiracy of silence in the face of the obvious as somewhat amusing. As Tony Blair put it in a wry aside while addressing a joint session of Congress in the 1990s, "It's hard to worry too much about a country that can solve so many of its problems with a higher tax on petrol."

History counsels that changes in tax structures are ordinarily catalyzed by crisis. This time it won't be war, but the triple threat of the baby boom's retirement, the anxiety created by globalization, and the threat of environmental disaster that spurs America's move to higher and different kinds of taxes.

Which still leaves one question: Who's actually going to start the conversation about raising taxes, and where will they begin?

11

ONLY THE (LOWER) UPPER CLASS CAN SAVE US FROM INEQUALITY

"We should tax the shit out of these guys."

That's what a well-known and otherwise mild-mannered Ivy League economics professor (and member of the Lower Upper Class) told me regarding the sums that CEOs, private equity honchos, and assorted other banking and financial types have been earning. "My argument is that these super-rich people are earning classic rents," he explained. To economists, "rent" refers to the difference between what a factor of production is paid and what it would need to be paid to remain in its current use. Rents are present in situations where some form of market power is exercised—as in monopoly power, political power, even "star power." Say a football star is paid $100,000 a week to play for his team when he'd be willing to do it for $20,000. The excess $80,000 is "rent." Since reducing rents doesn't affect what people actually choose to do, economists say they can be taxed without hurting the real economy.

This was the professor's point. "These CEOs would do exactly what they did if they were paid half of what they're paid," he said. "The deals in Wall Street would go through if the investment bankers earned half. So these are classic rents and we can tax them to take the edge off of today's growing inequality. I find it more productive not to argue the question of whether the system is 'rigged,' or whether their compensation is really produced by 'market forces,' but to ask whether the supply of those services would be any less if those people were taxed at a fifty percent marginal rate." His voice was rising on the phone, betraying a touch of anger. "To me that's the crucial issue—these earnings are pure rents!" he went on. *So we should tax the shit out of these guys!"*

Yes, it's a fancier argument than your average Lower Upper might make. And it may seem far-fetched to think the rebellion against extreme inequality will be led by tenured professors ready to march beyond the ivory tower—or for that matter by posh Lower Upper professionals roiling with resentment in their six-room Park Avenue apartments. But the truth is there's an opening for a "comeuppance agenda" aimed at the ultrarich that would be immensely satisfying to Lower Uppers—and which would fit nicely with a security and opportunity agenda for everyone else.

PROGRESSIVISM: THE SEQUEL

The brewing revolt of the Lower Uppers is an instance of history repeating itself. Indeed, the historian Richard Hofstadter focused on precisely this group in his classic 1955 history of the Progressive movement, *The Age of Reform*. "It is my thesis that men of this sort" helped lead the movement, he wrote, "not because of economic deprivations but because they were victims of an upheaval in status that took place in the United States during the closing decades of the nineteenth and the early years of the twentieth century. . . . In a strictly economic sense, these men were not growing poorer as a class, but their wealth and power were being dwarfed by comparison with the new eminences of wealth and power. They were less important, and they knew it."

Hoftstadter noted that the professional class felt it had "been ousted almost entirely by new men of the crudest sort." "If our civilization is destroyed," wrote Henry Demarest Lloyd in *Wealth Against Commonwealth,* an 1894 appraisal of the robber barons, "it will not be by . . . barbarians from below. Our barbarians come from above."

The journalist Walter Weyl's observations of social resentments in *The New Democracy,* written in 1914, sound uncannily like sentiments we hear a century later. "To a considerable extent the plutocracy is hated not for what it does but for what it is," wrote Weyl.

> Our over-moneyed neighbors cause a relative deflation of our personalities. . . . Everywhere . . . we meet the millionaire's good and evil works, and we seem to resent the one as much as the other. Our jogging horses are passed by their high powered automobiles. We are obliged to take their dust. . . . We are developing new types of destitutes—the automobileless, the yachtless, the Newport-cottage-less. The subtlest of luxuries become necessities, and their loss is bitterly resented. The discontent of today reaches very high in the social scale. . . . Our eminences have become higher and more dazzling. . . . Although lawyers, doctors, engineers, architects and professional men make larger salaries than ever before, the earning of one hundred thousand dollars a year by one lawyer impoverishes by comparison the thousands of lawyers who scrape by on a thousand a year [a healthy sum in 1914].

We are obliged to take their dust. Conditions like these, especially when wealth seems ill gotten or wildly out of proportion to the contribution those earning it have made to society, create kindling for popular brushfires ignited from above. In our own era, the most pertinent (if now tarnished) early sign of this trend was the nerve struck by Eliot Spitzer in his days as a crusading attorney general, before his unsavory fall. When Spitzer took on the shocking greed of men like Richard Grasso, who felt he deserved hundreds of millions of dollars for running the nonprofit New York Stock Exchange, or corrupt investment bankers who made millions touting stocks they privately knew were dogs, the public's outrage and its support for Spitzer's actions were close to universal. In 1906 a similar crusade against corrupt CEOs in New York's insurance industry vaulted Charles Evans Hughes, a Lower Upper lawyer, to the governor's mansion, and eventually to the Supreme Court and the Republican presidential nomination. Hughes's nationally reported investigation served as a harbinger for an era of progressive reform.

As was the case one hundred years ago, however, the broader reform possibilities inherent in these developments do not spring merely from Lower Upper resentment or from popular revulsion at industry excess. They stem instead *from the way the experience of humiliation and loss of status at the hands of the ultrarich expands the boundaries of Lower Upper empathy.* The energy for real reform is the altered outlook of this influential segment of society. "If the professional groups changed their ideas and took on new loyalties," Hofstadter wrote of that earlier time, "it was not in simple response to changes in the nature of the country's problems . . . but rather because they had become disposed to see things they had previously ignored and to agitate themselves about things that had previously left them unconcerned. . . . As men who were in their own way suffering from the incidence of the status revolution, they were able to understand and empathize with the problems of other disinherited groups."

FEELING THEIR PAIN:
LOWER UPPERS MEET LUCK

With their noses pressed up against the glass of better clubs, homes, schools, planes, and resorts to which they no longer have access, today's hard-working Lower Uppers are experiencing the bitter taste of diminishment. The flip side of their loss of faith in "merit" will be a deeper appreciation for the role of luck in life. This awakening will have powerful political implications.

Luck is a shorthand term for those things that shape our lives that are entirely outside our control. In one sense it refers to the pre-birth lottery: a person's inherited genes, race, wealth, looks, brains, and talents; the values and character of the family in which a person grows up; the education that comes (or doesn't come) in this pack-age. Where you happen to be born is also critical here; whether you enter the world in Boston or Baghdad will go far in determining your life's possibilities. All these factors are outside our control. We can't take credit for them or be blamed for them. It's this sense of luck that inspired the famous thought experiment described in the philosopher John Rawls's 1972 book *A Theory of Justice.* The way to create the rules for a just society, Rawls argued, is to first imagine everyone in an "original position" behind a prebirth "veil of igno-rance," where no one knows what their own traits will be— whether they will be rich or poor, beautiful or plain, smart or less so, talented or not, healthy or unwell. Then you'd see what kind of social order people would agree in advance was fair if they couldn't know what place they themselves were destined to occupy in it. From this vantage point, of course, qualities we often consider part of "merit" are really traceable to luck, since a person's brains, and to some extent their character (at least when they're young), are shaped by factors over which they have no influence.

In another sense, "luck" refers to things like natural disasters, events that befall people that their own actions and behavior can't affect. From the point of view of many Americans losing ground today, the accelerating effects of globalization and rapid technological change represent a searing case of bad luck.

Needless to say, the question of whether and how society should respond to luck's dominion has major implications for public policy. It's the bedrock dividing line in the moral outlooks of individuals and in rival political philosophies. Conservatives, worried that an honest admission of luck's role would sanction radical, economy-killing egalitarianism, have always ended up downplaying or ignoring luck. Liberals, while deeply concerned with luck, have typically been unwilling to craft efforts to ease the burden of bad luck in ways that preserve the best of capitalist innovation and the virtues of individual responsibility.

In the modern era, however, one of the most influential segments of society has largely stood apart from these questions, acting as if they didn't matter. Lower Uppers have been largely blind to the role of luck because it has been drilled into them, from their earliest successes jumping through the hoops of the American meritocracy, that they weren't "lucky" at all. They were "smart." They were "good." They were "hard-working."

Now that their second-tier status is awakening them to the fragility of "merit" as the source of their self-esteem and as the basis for where they "deserve" to stand in society, Lower Uppers will start seeing luck's hand elsewhere. They'll see it not only in their own story or in the fate of the ultrarich above them, but in the destiny of millions of their countrymen, now buffeted and struggling with rapid economic change. They'll be open to fresh appeals about what these powerful forces outside people's control should mean for society's basic arrangements. As a result they'll become stronger voices for equal opportunity, and for some set of minimal protections appropriate for citizens of a wealthy nation like the United States. Like their Progressive Era predecessors, and like our angry professor at the start of this chapter, they'll also see justice (and take satisfaction) in asking the ultrarich to kick a little more into the pot to make this happen.

For a glimpse of what the future will sound like, listen to Robert Crandall, the legendary, tough-as-nails CEO of American Airlines who retired in 1997 before upper end income really took off, and who spoke to the *New York Times* about his concerns in 2007:

> He is speaking out now, he said, because he no longer has to worry that his "radical views" might damage the reputation of American or that of the companies he served until recently as a director. The nation's corporate chiefs would be living far less affluent lives, Mr. Crandall said, if fate had put them in, say, Uzbekistan instead of the United States, "where they are the beneficiaries of a market system that rewards a few people in extraordinary ways and leaves others behind."

"The way our society equalizes incomes," Crandall went on to argue, "is through much higher taxes than we have today. There is no other way."

YOUR CROWN, MY LADY?

Historians caution that it is rare for economic resentment to get politically mobilized. To gauge the prospects for such a backlash, history counsels a look at several criteria, says Michael McGerr of Indiana University, one of the leading contemporary historians of the Progressive Era. One is to ask whether the ultrarich are taking steps to try to establish themselves as a kind of permanent nobility or plutocracy. (Might the drive to eliminate the estate tax fit here?) Another is whether the ultrarich are living in ways that are fundamentally alien to the rest of the country, or show radically different values than Americans hold generally. Compared to the pre–Progressive Era we may not have reached that point; even today's gaudiest hedge fund soirees are no match for the costume ball thrown by Cornelia Bradley-Martin at the Waldorf in the depression winter of 1897, when New York City's police commissioner, Theodore Roosevelt, ordered 250 cops to close down the block around the hotel (where his wife was dancing inside) for fear that "anarchists" might be moved by this symbol of excess to riot. Nor do we yet see anything quite like the Vanderbilt family, whose women took to wearing crowns in public to connote their superiority (and not just little tiaras, apparently, but heavy duty headgear). McGerr also notes that these social dynamics can take a generation to gestate; Gilded Age excesses that began in the 1870s and 1880s didn't ripen into something that provoked a political backlash until twenty-five years later.

But the night is young, as they say. And in the Internet age everything moves faster, including history itself. Karl Marx thought the envy of the proletariat would bring capitalism down. He was wrong. But before long the envy of the merely affluent will help pull today's übercapitalists down a peg or two even as it pulls everyone else up, thereby taking the edge off today's extreme inequality.

12

ONLY BETTER LIVING
CAN SAVE SAGGING PAYCHECKS

The American dream of upward mobility remains real for poor immigrants whose grit and hard work fuel their rise. But, as we've seen, native born Americans now face a triple whammy: the economy is not growing as fast; the benefits from growth are not as broadly distributed; and millions of people aren't earning as much as their parents did. All of which raises a question: What toll will this take on the American psyche? Is the land of can-do optimism destined to become a grumpier, unhappier nation? Over the next few years the answer will almost certainly be yes, because more Americans will feel financially squeezed or threatened, and they'll be frustrated and angry about it. But in the longer term there's great hope, as technology works its magic and we're forced by events to develop a saner view of what matters in life. A shorter way to put this is that "only better living can save sagging paychecks." Technological progress will continuously make many of the material features of ordinary life better and cheaper, even as sagging earnings lead more of us to seek pleasure and happiness beyond the consumer culture altogether.

In assessing the link between economic performance and the national mood, the first thing to note is that when it comes to the level of material abundance Americans enjoy, even those losing ground today live more comfortably than almost anyone else on earth. It may be small comfort for those feeling squeezed, but it's true: most of humanity would be thrilled to trade places with America's "struggling middle class."

Beyond this, it's also clear that technological advance has already been easing the pain. Recent research suggests, for example, that the widening income gap masks a narrowing difference in the actual consumption experiences of the rich and the rest of us. Consider the leveling one sees in the market for transport and appliances. "You no longer need to be a Vanderbilt to own a refrigerator or a car," *The Economist* reported in 2008, adding drily that "refrigerators are now all but universal in America, even though refrigerator inequality continues to grow." Their point is that the difference between the rich man's $11,000 Sub-Zero "monument to food preservation" and the poor man's discount-store fridge is smaller than the onetime difference between being able to have fresh meat and milk and having none. Likewise, the difference between driving an affordable used car and a lavish new BMW is tiny compared to the difference between driving on roads and, say, walking or bicycling. "The vast spread of prices," the magazine concludes, "often distracts from a narrowing range of experience."

In addition, some economists point out that today's lower reported earnings do not necessarily mean that people are living less well than their parents. What does this mean? It is often observed that the average American or European today lives better than royalty did a century or so ago—in terms of life span, general health, medical care, food, drink, transportation, communications, and even shelter. Now, as the twenty-first century unfolds, average homes get bigger and more perfectly climate controlled; computers, cheaper and faster; entertainment options, almost literally infinite; cars, safer; cell phones, more versatile and ubiquitous; and so forth. And this is just the start: we're on the edge of an era in which new technologies in medicine, information, materials, communications, and transport will bring quantum leaps in human choice, comfort, and health.

Can such advances offset the anxiety and instability posed by stagnant wages? Well, to some extent we've been running a low voltage version of this experiment for the last thirty years, since wages for most Americans began to stall, and guess what: people haven't revolted. Liberals tend to be mystified by this fact—shaking voters by the shoulders as if to say, "Why aren't you more upset? Where's the outrage?" But for all the left's just concern that the gains from growth have been tilted toward the best off, the truth is that continued technological progress has helped make this maldistribution more palatable. That doesn't mean we shouldn't take steps to reverse these inequities through public policy progress; we should. But technological advance is as or more important to improving the human condition.

Our measures of such advances are also imperfect. For example, the fact that medicine performs more miracles, or that cell phones and iPods offer ubiquitous convenience in communications and music, is not always fully captured by the official economic data. Imagine a wildly expensive iPod equivalent thirty years ago, for instance, something that only very rich people could have had custom engineered just for them; now it is available to almost everybody. Economists say this should be reflected in the data as a decline in price—the opposite of inflation. If price levels are going down to the extent such improvements in quality and new products are occurring over time, and for some reason we're not capturing this adequately in our current measures (because it can be tricky to figure out), then people's real (that is, inflation-adjusted) incomes may be somewhat higher today than we think. If so, that's good news.

The bigger, badder news, however, is that any potential undermeasurement of today's technology-adjusted quality of life can't offset the broader trajectory of American stagnation, because for years the costs of key features of middle-class life, particularly housing, college, and health care (and more recently energy and food), have unequivocally soared far faster than median incomes. This situation won't be remedied overnight.

WHAT PRICE HAPPINESS?

So what happens in the meantime? While we wait for a blend of technology, market forces, and new government policy to bring these critical elements of middle-class life back within reach, the question, if you care about the American temperament, is the ancient one: Does money buy happiness? While a priest will reply differently than a financial planner, and it's hard to generalize about 300 million moods, the short answer, at least based on the latest research, is "yes, but."

Economists and psychologists used to believe that above some minimal threshold of income—around $10,000 a year—more earnings didn't lead people to report higher levels of satisfaction with their lives. Instead, people's happiness tended to depend on their income relative to others they viewed as a reference point—which helps explain the distemper of so many Lower Uppers, who by every objective measure are doing extremely well. As Bertrand Russell wisely observed in *The Conquest of Happiness* in 1930, "The habit of thinking in terms of comparison is a fatal one." The most recent research, however, suggests that absolute levels of income do indeed play a major role in how happy people say they are. Richer Americans tell pollsters they are much happier than do poorer Americans. People in rich countries say they're happier than do those in poorer ones.

Hold the presses, you're probably thinking—this isn't exactly surprising news. Moreover, common sense suggests both views have merit: we care about how we're doing relative to others, but also tend to be happier, all things being equal, with more resources at our disposal. The trouble is that as a growing segment of workers' incomes sag, more Americans will feel worse off in both the relative and the absolute sense. This portends a darker national mood in the near future.

Still, as people's expectations adjust to new circumstances, this should change. In other situations in which people experience a reversal of fortune—such as disability or divorce—the initial shock, loss, and disappointment eventually yield to a new psychological baseline from which people move forward. Humanity's amazing adaptability in the face of whatever life throws at us serves us well.

This is especially hopeful given that we know that human well-being depends on much more than material things. The sad, lonely rich man is a commonplace. Good health is the obvious first determinant of a positive outlook on life. Recent research also shows that the more full our lives are with intimate relationships and companionship, and with engaging leisure and spiritual activities (everything from fishing and listening to music to visiting friends and going to church), the happier we tend to be at any level of income.

The economist Alan Krueger of Princeton University, who has helped lead some of this new research, says that "in the past the American tendency has been to buy new goods and consume and go into debt, and to under-appreciate interacting with friends and simple pleasures." People spend less time on these simple pleasures than they used to, studies show; instead we've been working longer hours (trying to keep our incomes up) and then zoning out more in front of the television.

The economic challenges ahead will spark a renaissance of

interest in these less material sources of meaning and happiness, and for many a flight from the consumer culture altogether. To mix metaphors and clichés, those who can't keep up with the Joneses will simply leave the rat race. Time with friends and loved ones will become more cherished. The craving for community will deepen. And curiosities like today's nascent "slow movement," which cheerleads for (among other things) longer meals savored with loved ones and a quieter pace of life in general, will expand from a niche lifestyle to a broader force in the culture. If this evolution in values sounds almost European, it's because at this crossroads there is much that Europe can teach us. Jeremy Rifkin, the author of *The European Dream,* which favorably compares the Continent's approach to life to America's, notes that Europe emphasizes "community relationships over individual autonomy, cultural diversity over assimilation, quality of life over the accumulation of wealth, sustainable development over unlimited material growth," and "deep play over unrelenting toil." Sounds pretty appealing. While we may not get eight weeks' paid vacation and three-hour siestas, the average European's superior talent for enjoying life will be an inspiration as we navigate uncertain economic times.

SAVED BY THE GEEK

In the longer run, of course, technology will save us. Ray Kurzweil, the visionary computer scientist and inventor, paints a dazzling picture of a world not long from now with almost unimaginable potential. "As powerful as information technology is today," Kurzweil wrote recently,

> we will make another billion-fold increase in capability (for the same cost) over the next 25 years. That's because information technology builds on itself—we are continually using the latest tools to create the next so they grow in capability at an exponential rate.

That doesn't just mean snazzier cellphones. It means that change will rock every aspect of our world. The exponential growth in computing speed will unlock a solution to global warming, unmask the secret to longer life and solve myriad other worldly conundrums.

Take energy. Today, 70 percent of it comes from fossil fuels, a nineteenth-century technology. According to Kurzweil, if we could capture just one ten-thousandth of the sunlight that falls on earth, we could meet all the world's energy needs. We can't do that now because solar panels still rely on relatively heavy, expensive, and inefficient technologies. But a new generation of panels based on nanotechnology, which (amazingly) controls matter via miniature devices that operate on a molecular scale, is beginning to surmount these hurdles. Within about twenty years, he says, solar energy will become an affordable answer, lowering the average person's energy bill even as it eases the danger of global warming.

Or take medicine, which only now, thanks to genetic research, is becoming viewed as a set of information processes. In one recent experiment, the fat insulin receptor was turned off in mice, which meant they were able to eat voraciously yet remain slim and live 20 percent longer. Countless drugs are now in the pipeline to unplug the genes that lead to obesity, cancer, heart disease, and more.

"The important point," says Kurzweil,

is this: Now that we can model, simulate and program biology just like we can a computer, it will be subject to the law of accelerating returns, a doubling of capacity in less than a year. These technologies will be more than a thousand times more capable in a decade, more than a million times more capable in two decades. We are now adding three months every year to human life expectancy, but . . . this will soon go into high gear. According to my models,

15 years from now we'll be adding more than a year each year to our remaining life expectancy. This is not a guarantee of living forever, but it does mean that the sands of time will start pouring in instead of only pouring *out*.

If Kurzweil and others are even a fraction right, we and our children are in for remarkable things. Doubtless these advances will raise myriad ethical challenges; the tension between health care haves and have-nots as biological advances are deployed first to the wealthy, for example, could be grist for a whole other book. Yet Kurzweil and his fellow geeks believe the breakthroughs ahead will ultimately have the greatest impact in lifting the world's poor.

Why am I lingering over this taste of what's to come? By way of suggesting that a generation of adjustment as poorer countries rise and technology reshapes work is not inconsistent with a better quality of life in America in the future, even for those who earn less. Beyond making sure that health care and pension security aren't linked to specific jobs, the answer to this seeming riddle is that technological innovation in products and services can continue to improve people's lives in ways that ultimately outpace wage strains. Promoting continued large-scale technical innovation will be even more important in an era when wages are at risk, because the wide dispersal of such advances is crucial for social peace. This means bigger investments in basic scientific research, and regulations that assure new discoveries are widely deployed. This will all pose a tricky political question as well: Is there any way to craft an optimistic message out of this "better living despite sagging wages" notion that would allow politicians to talk about these scenarios candidly and fend off calls for protectionism that would make matters worse? Or will our leaders need to resort to pretty public charades while privately counting on technology to work its magic? The odds favor the latter, but it's impossible to know. The answer will help determine how fraudulent our public discourse will be for at least a generation.

A final word on better living even in an era of sagging wages. Excellent public amenities—like city parks and recreation facilities—can make life better for ordinary people, just as technology can. If we're serious about preserving the social stability that underpins economic growth, the era ahead will thus require us finally to tackle the gap between what John Kenneth Galbraith famously called "private affluence and public squalor." I can't say this is "destined" to happen, like much else we've discussed. But it ought to.

13

ONLY A DOSE OF "NATIONALIZATION" CAN SAVE LOCAL SCHOOLS

When I asked Marc Tucker, who led the bipartisan New Commission on the Skills of the American Workforce, how he explains to people that America's fetish for local control is hurting us, he replied that he begins by asking a simple question: If it is true (as it is) that we have the second most costly K–12 education system among the major industrialized nations, and that our performance consistently places us between the middle and the bottom of the pack, would it not make sense, in looking for solutions to that problem, to examine the experiences of those countries that spend less and get more from their schools? "Having asked that rhetorical question," Tucker says, "I then point out that this system of local control that we have in the United States is almost unique compared to those countries that have high performance. Rather than making it the unquestioned assumption, one then has to defend holding on to a practice that is uncharacteristic of those countries that have the best performance.

"It's an industrial benchmarking argument," Tucker adds.

Horace Mann wouldn't have used this jargon back in 1843, but his determination to improve American educational practice by learning from the best in the world is poised to be repeated today. In Mann's time, the challenge was to embrace a bigger role for the states; nearly 170 years later, in an era of global competition, the challenge is to embrace a role for the nation that gives children a chance to thrive no matter where in America they happen to be born. This national leadership will finally be asserted (and welcomed) in the decade ahead as parents and officials wake up to the fact that *there is no other choice if we're serious about preserving our standard of living.*

No one will be able to say we didn't try everything else first. Think about it: since the publication of *A Nation at Risk* in 1983, we've had literally dozens of blue-ribbon reports laying out the problems and offering determined "action plans," countless court decrees meant to fix state funding inequities, fifty states playing around with idiosyncratic standards and testing regimes—and then the federal government tiptoeing sheepishly around the whole mess with a new layer of toothless, unfunded mandates gussied up in yet another hollow pledge to leave no child behind. What do we have to show for all this? A dropout epidemic, the most unjust system of school finance in the advanced world, sagging scores in international comparisons, and a teaching crisis in poor neighborhoods that is a moral and economic disgrace. As more showcases like the Beijing Olympics offer reminders that others are passing us by in terms of infrastructure investment, educational attainment, broadband connections, airport services, and other harbingers of future economic strength, it will finally dawn on a critical mass of Americans that the only way to get serious about excellence and equity in our schools is for the federal government to step up and make it happen. As a result, Uncle Sam in the years ahead will take on pivotal new roles in standards and finance, as well as in promoting educational innovation and a more cosmopolitan outlook among young people. Despite all the usual anti-Washington bloviating, these directions are now in the cards. Let's take them in turn.

The usual explanation for why national standards haven't been established in the United States is because the right hates "national" and the left hates "standards." But that's already changing. Two former Republican secretaries of education, Rod Paige and William Bennett, now support national standards and tests, writing in the *Washington Post* that "in a world of fierce economic competition, we can't afford to pretend that the current system is getting us where we need to go." On the Democratic side, the 2005 report of the education task force at the Center for American Progress (where I'm a senior fellow) included a call for voluntary national standards that states could opt to embrace. Yet when I spoke not long ago with CAP president John Podesta, a former chief of staff to President Clinton, he said he'd become convinced since the report was issued that people were now far ahead of the conventional wisdom in Washington, which holds that the only safe way to dodge the standards question is to hedge defensively about their being "optional" or "voluntary" or otherwise not really "national" at all.

Polling suggests he's right. An August 2007 survey done for Strong American Schools, an education campaign funded by the Gates and Broad foundations (which I advised), found that 63 percent of Americans thought there should be "national academic expectations and standards for students in all states," as opposed to 35 percent who felt "each state should be responsible for setting its own." Another survey for the campaign found that 81 percent of voters supported the concept of instituting uniform national standards in core subjects (including 53 percent who supported this "strongly"). A 2008 survey by the journal *Education Next* found not only overwhelming support for national standards and tests, but that Republicans liked the idea even more than Democrats. In one sense this won't represent a huge change, because de facto national education standards in some areas already exist, set indirectly by a handful of publishing giants whose textbooks (shaped largely by the desires of megastates California, Florida, and Texas) guide instruction in classrooms across the country. The question there-fore is not really "should we?" but "how best to?" Yes, there will be feuds along the way, but we'll eventually start by establishing some version of national standards and tests in grades three through twelve in core subjects—reading, math, and science, for starters—leaving more controversial subjects, like history, until we get our feet wet with the new regime.

NIXON NOW!

When it comes to finance, nowhere is it written in the Constitution that the federal government can contribute only 9 percent of K–12 spending. Once we start getting serious about preparing all chil-dren to thrive in an era of global competition, that will change. The most recent important official to look hard at this question was none other than Richard Nixon. That fact alone should shock us: it's been more than thirty-five years since we've had anything resembling a national debate about this massive "elephant in the room." Nixon's Commission on School Finance, headed by the chairman of Procter & Gamble, issued a report in 1972 that urged states to equalize funding disparities between districts, and offered a little federal cash to help. But bolder ideas were also in play. Nixon's commissioner of education, for example, said publicly that the federal government should pay 25 to 30 percent of the cost of public education. John Ehrlichman's staff weighed what one leak to the *New York Times* suggested could be Nixon's "education mas-terstroke": a new national value-added tax whose proceeds would be distributed to states that drastically reduced state and local prop-erty taxes while closing funding gaps among their districts.

Precise details are less important at this point than recognizing that something like Nixon's never-proposed property tax swap "masterstroke" offers the kind of fresh framework for school finance we'll move toward over time. The feds contributed $45 billion of the $488 billion total spent on K–12 schools in 2004–05 (the most recent data available). Going to 25 to 30 percent of today's overall tab via Nixonian revenue sharing would lift the federal contribution by roughly $80 billion to $100 billion a year in order to "buy down" equivalent amounts of state and local taxes. (Some extra federal money might be needed as well to sweeten the pot, round up the votes, and boost the poorest schools.)

Goodwin Liu of the University of California, Berkeley, has offered two useful principles to inform the evolving federal role. The first is to bring all states up to a certain guaranteed baseline of funding per pupil. To be eligible for such support, states would have to tax themselves at a certain minimal rate, to show some appropriate level of effort given the resources they have. Then, in those cases where states still fell short (because they were poorer), the feds would, in essence, compensate them for the shortfall. Another idea, applying above this minimum, would be for the federal government to help equalize the return a state gets on a given level of tax effort. Much of the variation in spending among states is not the result of differing tax effort, but because even with reasonably high levels of effort, some states (such as West Virginia) get low returns, because their wealth per child isn't high—unlike such states as Tennessee and Florida, which spend less because they prefer low taxes. The idea would be for the feds to make sure that if a state taxes itself at x rate it will get y return. "The federal role should not be an insurance policy for the states that want to spend less and have low taxes," says Liu. "It should be an insurance policy against low wealth."

One scenario to raise the federal contribution to 25 to 30 percent would be to adopt a Liu-style plan, which might cost $30 billion a year, and use the additional billions for conditional grants to states enabling some new "grand bargains" that boost school performance. For example, federal cash could be offered to lift teacher salaries substantially for high poverty schools, provided that states or districts (1) allow big pay differentials for high performing teachers or those in shortage specialties like math and science; (2) defer or eliminate tenure (or condition it on proven student achievement gains); and (3) make it easier to fire low performers. A federally financed initiative like this would let us pay top teachers up to $150,000 a year, attracting a new generation of talent to America's toughest classrooms. Hefty grants might also be offered to states that adopt new national standards, making them voluntary but perhaps via offers that states couldn't sensibly refuse. Furthermore, federal cash could help innovative, high performing charter school operators like KIPP or Green Dot to expand while also helping regular public schools replicate their model, which involves investment in longer school days and years as well as extra student supports. Support for state efforts to universalize preschool could also be thrown in. As you can see, once the feds start to move from 9 percent toward 30 percent of the K–12 dollar, the possibilities are enormous.

The federal government will also use a portion of its higher investment to pursue an R&D agenda more equal to the education sector's needs. As Chris Whittle, the founder of Edison Schools, has argued, it doesn't make sense that the feds spend $28 billion on basic research yearly at the National Institutes of Health, but only $260 million (or 1 percent of that) on R&D for education. Whittle argues persuasively that $4 billion a year on such innovation could begin "to move our schools—and our educational results—to another level, just as we moved from the candle to the light bulb, from the prop plane to the jet." Finally, where but at the national level will we insist that all American children develop the cosmopolitan outlook needed to thrive in a "flat world"? This might mean requiring fluency in a second language for high school graduation, as well as courses that expose students to the planet's myriad cultures and religions. In the twenty-first century it should not be left to the whim of a rural district in, say, Nebraska whether or not an American child has some minimal feel for the shrinking world she will share.

The directions we've just sketched are more or less foreordained; as the depth of our school system's failures become apparent in our showdown with rising economies abroad, the only real question is how long we'll take to adapt. The fate of school boards in this mix is more complicated and uncertain. The best course would be to scrap them. That's the impulse behind the growing drive for mayoral control of schools, though only a few major cities have thus far achieved it. While it's too soon to render a verdict, New York and Boston have used mayoral authority to sustain what are among the most far-reaching reform agendas in the country.

Every education reformer I spoke with, from liberal to conservative, said there would be no loss whatsoever if we woke up one day to discover that school boards had vanished. (It's hard to think of other institutions that inspire such consensus.) They also say that with 95,000 school board members as an active lobbying force, the chances of that happening anytime soon are nil. That means we need to find ways to recast school boards' role so they can do less damage.

WHAT WOULD HORACE DO?

As our school system evolves, it's vital that one seeming paradox is understood: *it is only by transcending traditional local control, and by getting serious about this new national role in standards and finance, that we can at last create genuine autonomy for local schools.* This autonomy should become the new definition of what we mean when we say "local control."

That's because schools operating under "local control" today are in reality controlled anywhere but locally. Spend time in them and you'll fast learn that principals don't "run" schools; they're compliance machines, making sure that federal, state, and district programs are legally administered. Their hands, and those of the teachers, are tied by an intricate puzzle of laws, program regulations, policies, and employment contracts that cover every minute of the day; the number of hours per day; the number of days in the year; the number and type of credits needed to graduate; hiring and teacher assignment; curriculum, course offerings, and textbooks; testing, promotion, and retention; class size; student behavior; discipline; health, safety, and civil rights; sex ed, driver's ed, meals, before- and after-school programs; and, of course, sports. On top of this byzantine multitiered set of compliance policies, the standards movement has now appended local, state, and federal levels of accountability policy that are not aligned. This leaves schools in the surreal position where they may get an award from their state for *high* performance even as they are targeted under federal guidelines for closure because of *low* performance. This happens in California all the time.

"If you visit schools in many other parts of the world," says Marc Tucker, "you're struck almost immediately . . . by a sense of autonomy on the part of the school staff and principal that you don't find in the United States." International studies have found the same thing: individual public schools in the United States have less autonomy than nationally directed schools in France. Research across forty-six countries by Ludger Woessmann of the University of Munich has shown that having a clear set of external standards to be judged by, combined with real discretion at the school level in how to get there, turns out to be the most effective way to run a school system, and the most satisfying for educators and parents. If you have strong external standards and don't have school autonomy, the results are mediocre. If you have strong autonomy, but no good external standards, you also have mediocre results. Only by measuring results well can we free educators to run effective schools that can also tailor key features of schooling to what parents want locally in a pluralistic society. In other words: we need to give schools one clear national set of expectations, free educators and parents to collaborate locally in whatever ways get results, *and get everything else out of the way.* New York City under Mayor Michael Bloomberg has been trying to move in this direction. An education reform commission set up by Governor Arnold Schwarzenegger laid out a similar blueprint for California. In the years ahead, the federal government will finally accelerate this agenda for the nation.

To his contemporaries in the 1840s, Horace Mann could be self-righteous and high-handed as he campaigned for public schools, acting as if America's destiny and superiority were self-evident. But if he could be pigheaded in a good cause, Mann was also intellectually honest and curious. When he went to Prussia, he opened his mind.

Everyone who cares about schools in America needs to take a mental trip to Prussia today. Nationalizing our schools a little is antithetical to every cultural tradition in the United States, save the one that matters most: our capacity to renew ourselves to meet the challenges of a new day. Once upon a time a national role in retirement security was anathema; then suddenly, after the Depression, there was Social Security. Once a federal role in health care would have been damned as socialism, yet federal spending now accounts for half of all the dollars devoted to health care in the United States, with more certain to come in the years ahead. When it comes to schools, there has likewise always been a tension between the desire to improve the life chances of more children by involving higher levels of authority, and the primordial American distrust of central government. But the truth is we started down this road even on schooling a long time ago. In the years ahead we'll move to finish the job.

14

ONLY LESSONS FROM ABROAD CAN SAVE AMERICAN IDEALS

When great American companies think about improving their performance, they benchmark their operations against the best in the world. That's how they refine their standards of excellence and find new ideas to adapt. But in America's public conversation this commonsense approach is often trumped by mindless snobbery. "You want us to look at what Singapore is doing on health care or Finland is doing on teacher training?" the attitude seems to be. "That may be fine for a benevolent dictatorship in Asia or a tiny sauna-loving tundra—but this is friggin' *America!*" This phony patriotic arrogance is one of the dark sides of American exceptionalism, and it blinds us to good ideas. It's a luxury America can't afford in the twenty-first century, and one that luckily we'll soon be forced to scrap.

As America's dominance in the global economy yields to greater economic parity with Europe and a rising Asia, our knee-jerk condescension will erode. Instead, it will become clear that we can only preserve American ideals by taking a cue from countries that do a better job of combining growth with equity and social mobility. This doesn't mean successful foreign approaches can be transplanted without adapting them to our unique culture, or that everything that works elsewhere will make sense here. But on many of the challenges we've discussed, we'll find we have much to learn from the world.

It won't be the first time. Our political institutions were partly adapted from what our founders deemed impressive about Britain's parliament and judiciary. Our system of higher education was modeled after the great German universities of the late nineteenth century. Somewhere along the line between World War II and today we lost our instinct for plucking the best ideas from wherever they originate and began to think all wisdom resides with us. In business it took shattering crises like the one faced by the auto industry in the 1970s and 1980s to wake us up to the fact that better mousetraps were being built elsewhere. Though our public institutions won't face the same literal threat of going out of business if they don't adapt, they'll bend to the breaking point as key public functions in America prove similarly uncompetitive. Obvious instances of smart ideas from abroad that can help us move past Dead Ideas here include a more limited role for employers in managing and funding health care; consistent national standards in education; raising taxes on energy while lowering them on corporations; and even savoring lovingly prepared meals with friends and family more often. But this only scratches the surface. A few quick examples illustrate the range of activities on which we'll usefully go to school overseas as our parochial outlook becomes more cosmopolitan.

IT'S THE TEACHERS, STUPID

A landmark 2008 report by McKinsey & Company (where I serve as an adviser) that benchmarked the best school systems in the world came to a conclusion that should seem obvious but, at least in the United States, is not taken seriously: "The quality of an education system cannot exceed the quality of its teachers." American schools, especially those in poorer neighborhoods, typically recruit teachers from the bottom third of the college class, because teaching isn't a career that most top students find attractive. Not so elsewhere. Take Singapore, which stands near the top in math and science performance. The key to their success is being selective in recruiting and training teachers. Only one in six people who apply to become teachers are accepted; they're drawn from the top third of the class. Applicants must ace literacy tests, because the authorities find a strong link between the teachers' own literacy and student achievement. Three veteran principals grill each applicant for the prestigious teacher training program at Singapore's National Institute of Education, probing for passion, attitude, and charisma. Those accepted are put on the payroll of the Ministry of Education and actually get a salary while they're trained. This is a system, needless to say, that cherishes teachers.

Finland, another top-ranked school system, is even more selective, with ten applicants competing for every slot in the universities that train teachers. Why did Finland focus on classroom instruction as it reformed its schools in the 1970s and 1980s? "To provide equal opportunities in life for everyone," says Pekka Himanen, a philosopher who is one of Finland's leading young intellectuals and reformers. Himanen says a great education assures that a child's chances in life don't depend on "an accident of birth." Sounds like an all-American ideal.

Or consider the United Kingdom, which dramatically upgraded the status of teachers with pay hikes and a national marketing campaign that in just five years took teaching from a perceived backwater for people with few other options to the first choice among professions for college graduates. Starting teacher salaries, meanwhile, tend to be well above average incomes in countries with high performing schools; in the United States it remains well below. The overall contrast couldn't be more stark; many teacher's colleges here accept virtually anyone who applies, while only lip service has been paid to enhancing the pay and status of teaching as a profession.

School lessons from abroad go beyond teacher quality. Sweden and the Netherlands, for example, boast comprehensive systems of school choice in which the government lets parents choose the school their child will attend, with public money following the child. In Holland public money goes even to private and religious schools, so long as they meet certain rules for teaching standard subjects. While the two systems are naturally touted by the American right, U.S. conservatives overlook their other central feature: in both countries, every student receives identical per pupil funding, making these systems dramatically fairer than our own, where gaps of between $5,000 and $10,000 per pupil are common. In other advanced countries, equity in school funding is a core national value—indeed, Dutch students who are disadvantaged get extra resources, because the authorities believe they need more to succeed. One Dutch official told me he was shocked to learn of the funding gaps among schools and students in the United States; Holland would never tolerate such disparities, he said. Sweden and Holland have modeled a pairing of choice *and* equity from which our country could learn.

"FLEXICURITY"

Denmark's labor market model, known by the buzzword "flexicurity," may offer another source of inspiration for America in the years ahead. The idea is straightforward: Danes aim to combine the kind of *flexible* labor markets that assure a dynamic economy with the kind of *security* that helps workers welcome rather than resist economic change. On the one hand, Denmark has been determined to steer clear of the American free market extreme, in which the absence of various protections means that workers are thrown to the wind when companies or industries go through tough times—which leads workers, naturally enough, to fight change with everything they've got. Yet Denmark also seeks to avoid the stasis of the classic European model, in which rules that make it hard or costly for firms to fire employees makes them wary of hiring people in the first place. Down this road lie the higher unemployment and resistance to innovation that have plagued many European economies. In place of these skewed models, "flexicurity" strikes a new balance—freeing firms to adapt their labor force to changing business conditions while the nation commits to easing the transition for citizens caught in declining industries or occupations. The result is labor peace, low unemployment, and an ethic of business innovation, buffered by extraordinary public investments in retraining programs, wage subsidies, and unemployment insurance that typically covers around 95 percent of lost wages.

None of this happened in Denmark overnight; the system has been shaped by decades of negotiation and a sense of shared purpose among labor, management, and government. According to the author and columnist Robert Kuttner, who has studied the Danish model, it also depends on spending 4.5 percent of GDP on these various labor market programs, which would come to $600 billion a year in the United States. Yet the attitudinal change this investment buys is striking. "We need to convince Danish industry to do *more* outsourcing," one union leader says (emphasis added). What he means is that Danish multinationals should boost their competitiveness by sending routine jobs to developing countries while keeping higher value, higher paying jobs in Denmark. That's better for Danish workers and for Danish multinationals. With a mind-set like this, it's little wonder Denmark was recently ranked the third most competitive economy in the world by the World Economic Forum, after the United States and Switzerland.

IT'S ALL IN YOUR HEAD

Finally, consider market-based universal health care, something both Switzerland and the Netherlands have managed to pioneer. Both cover everyone using private insurers, and they do so for much less cost—10 percent of GDP for the Dutch and 12 percent for Switzerland, compared to 16 percent in the United States, where we still leave 50 million people uninsured. They also boast better health outcomes than we do, even when compared to states with similar demographics, such as Connecticut and Massachusetts. Sicker people in both countries are pursued as customers by private insurers—rather than shunned, as they are in the United States—because health plans are paid more for sick enrollees via a government-designed system of "risk adjustment." The Swiss and Dutch achievements are important because critics often act as if fully socialized systems, like those in Great Britain and Canada, are the inevitable result of any drive for universal coverage. In fact, as Switzerland and the Netherlands show, it is perfectly possible to cover everyone and take the burden off employers without any such "big government takeover."

There's more. Most advanced nations make university education affordable (or free) for good students who meet entry standards and can do the work. American national policy is to force middle and lower income students to graduate with mountains of debt. Isn't that crazy? Singapore's mandatory worker savings plans generate huge pools of cash for domestic investment while assuring retirement security for citizens. We don't have to ban chewing gum or opposition parties (as they do in Singapore) to see that there's real power in making sure that every citizen has access to the miracle of compound interest. (And while we're at it, let's learn how Singapore delivers first-world health care quality while spending just 5 percent of the GDP!) Sweden gives cash allowances to new fathers who take some time off from work, helping explain why you see more dads pushing strollers in Stockholm. Sounds civilized to me. I could go on, but you get the idea. It's a big, wide world out there and we need to get busy seeing what we can learn. Ideas from abroad won't be a panacea, but they'll open our minds to different ways of achieving what citizens of most wealthy nations want in life.

In the end, the great virtue of seeing how other countries approach these matters won't come from any specific idea we'll want to copy, but from the broader observation we'll come away with: most other nations actually have a strategy for what they're trying to accomplish for their economy and for their people that leaders across business, labor, government, and civic society can articulate. That's just not the case in America; we're the epitome of having no strategy at all. Let me be clear: having a shared national strategy isn't the same as renewing old fights from the 1980s about "industrial policy." I'm not talking about government "picking winners and losers" among industries. I'm talking about leaders from different sectors sitting around a table, assessing the challenges facing the country given the realities of the global economy, and devising ways to achieve commonsense goals for our citizens to which all segments of society make some contribution and from which all derive some benefit. It's the absence of *any* economic vision or strategy that makes America truly unique and truly vulnerable today. At present we're a collection of isolated economic players and interest groups in the grip of Dead Ideas that leave us blind to what's happening, and unable to act on any notion of shared purpose.

15

FROM DEAD TO
DESTINED IDEAS

In 1932, as America sank toward the depths of the Depression, pres-idential candidate Franklin Delano Roosevelt was maddeningly vague about his ideas for a "new deal" to lift the economy. But on one thing he was clear. As he barnstormed the country, Roosevelt attacked President Herbert Hoover's reckless budget deficits and promised to slash government spending to balance the books. Once in office, Roosevelt turned around and became the biggest-spending purveyor of red ink the country had ever seen.

What happened? Was Roosevelt a liar? I prefer to think of his flip-flop as a matter of "responsible demagoguery"—saying what he felt he had to say to get elected, while remaining privately com-mitted to doing what the country needed him to do to tackle its problems. In this notion lies a glimpse of how America will move past today's Dead Ideas in the decade ahead.

Though I would prefer it to be otherwise, the journey from Dead to Destined Ideas almost certainly won't come through rational public debate and consideration, because lovely as that sounds, it isn't the way our system works. Indeed, it's hard to imagine some of tomorrow's Destined Ideas—such as the need for substantially higher taxes, or the ways that even Americans who face stagnant incomes can still thrive—ever being honestly discussed in an election campaign.

But that doesn't mean America's leadership class won't come to recognize what needs to happen and act nonetheless. That's what Franklin Roosevelt did. It's what George H. W. Bush did when he reneged on his "read my lips" pledge to raise taxes in 1990, angering his core supporters and jeopardizing his reelection prospects. But the most relevant and intriguing recent example of "responsible demagoguery" was Arnold Schwarzenegger's major health care initiative in California in 2007.

Schwarzenegger's entire reelection campaign in 2006 was based on his pledge that he would not raise taxes; his endless mantra on the stump was that his Democratic opponent was just lusting to raise taxes to fund harebrained liberal schemes like universal health care. Two months after Schwarzenegger's landslide victory, what did he turn around and propose? Tax increases to pay for universal health coverage! No one batted an eye. Schwarzenegger's plan eventually went down to defeat, but not for lack of trying; the fight, and a Republican governor's understanding of the need to wage it, is a harbinger of what's ahead.

To some extent, of course, the gap between words and actions is a perennial (and depressing) feature of politics. But when we're at the exhausted edge of one set of ideas about economic life and another set is struggling to be born, the moral status of political deception becomes a subtler thing to judge. That's because *politicians win power by appealing to voters within the prevailing contours of debate.* Ask any political professional: elections are not the time to try to change people's minds about important matters. They're about communicating how your candidates' values and ideas fit with those ideas that *voters already hold.* If Lincoln had made the elimination of slavery the centerpiece of his campaign, there would be no Lincoln Memorial in Washington today, because he never would have gotten out of Illinois. If Franklin Roosevelt had shocked conventional sensibilities by pledging to run big deficits to spur the economy, he might have blown his chance for a big win against an unpopular incumbent. Today we find ourselves in a similar position, in which *the actual direction the country is bound to take is outside the permissible boundaries of public discussion.* The trick for those aspiring to leadership at such moments is to square the charades they must resort to in order to win power with the integrity to do what's right once they have it. The psychic strain this imposes on a human being is one of the reasons public service should be considered a sacrifice. (Though for most politicians, the will to power seems to come with related hormones that suppress the discomfort these conflicts would produce in normal people.)

It's also why character ultimately matters most in elections. At some level, voters know that politicians tell us what we want to hear; what we have to judge through the scrim of pandering is who has the mettle to make us eat our spinach afterward, if that's what we need to do. Unfortunately there's no sure way in advance to tell the responsible demagogue from the ordinary variety. Democracy in this sense is a permanent exercise of faith.

Still, the logic of reform is clear. Yes, it's true that we won't get big honest election debates on America's Dead Ideas, because that's not what happens in democracies. But a dishonest public life doesn't mean that our leaders won't be ready to do what has to be done. In the end what really matters is which ideas have currency in the minds of the people who run the country, regardless of whether they're prepared to say them out loud at first. So long as our leaders get the right ideas in their heads, and enough of the rest of us form a constituency that makes politicians feel safe pursuing them, we'll get where we need to go.

Seen in this context, the question comes down to this: Who will put the new ideas in our leaders' heads, and who will galvanize the new constituency? Though the pressure of events will shortly force all of us to rethink, this isn't some purely deterministic process, or a matter of divine revelation. In every transition like this, someone or some group has to lead the conversation. This time—drum roll, please—business executives will form the vanguard of the new creed.

IDEOLOGY AS LUXURY, CEO AS STATESMAN

Why do I predict this? Because at bottom, the coming transition from Dead to Destined Ideas will represent the triumph of pragmatism over ideology. This pragmatic sensibility has been in strikingly short supply in recent economic debates. Critics of national security policy in the 1990s like to say America acted as if it were on a "holiday from history," letting petty concerns (like the Monica Lewinsky scandal) divert us while terrorists plotted their strike. Yet in a broader sense, the entire economic era since World War II has been a holiday for the United States from the concerns and duties that more "normal" countries take for granted. In retrospect, one of the debilitating luxuries of this holiday has been our freedom to indulge in symbolic, ideologically charged political debates shaped by Dead Ideas, at least when it came to the economy; the absence of serious foreign competition or of accelerating technology that posed threats to the living standards of many Americans meant the economic machine could pretty much roll onward, whatever the politicians were blathering about.

Those days are over. Instead, we're entering a period when the ideological squabbling that's been so pointless and dispiriting will give way to a new pragmatic consensus, because the stakes of getting economic policy right will be much higher. We saw a glimpse of this pragmatic future in the instant jettisoning of free-market

convictions among people like President Bush and Treasury Secretary Hank Paulson when the credit crunch threatened catastrophe
in the fall of 2008. More such "awakenings" lie ahead. "Behold, my
son, with how little wisdom the world is governed!" ran the counsel
of Axel Oxenstierna, a Swedish statesman in the seventeenth century. This memorable remark has two meanings. In one sense the
Swede was simply saying, "Look at what idiots are running things!"
In another sense, though, he was offering a deeper observation
about how small a quantity of wise governance is actually required
to keep the human enterprise on track. Since shortly after World
War II, our economic life has been a blessed illustration of this
insight. Now we've reached the point when the American economy
can no longer succeed on autopilot; we need wiser governance.

To get it, America desperately needs a powerful, commonsense
constituency to force the questions and ideas we've discussed to
the top of the public agenda. Business is poised to fill this void. By
instinct and temperament the sector is clear-eyed and unsentimen-
tal. It prefers pragmatic results to ideology, and it has the clout to
be heard. The global reach of American enterprise means that
executives are among the first to see the threats that rising economies pose to business as usual in the United States. They see the
amazing new infrastructure in Shanghai, the superior broadband
network in Korea, India's hungry corps of engineers, Germany's
huge edge in solar energy. Their cosmopolitan outlook means
they're among the first to grasp how much we can learn from developments elsewhere. And business's need for an educated workforce
and a burgeoning middle class of consumers obviously gives it a profound stake in American economic success.

But for several reasons, business is not playing a leadership role
in shaping America's direction today. The first is simply lack of time
and focus. I can attest from my experience as a management consultant that most top executives and boards haven't thought

through what all these intersecting trends mean for the country as a whole; they're too busy coping with what these trends mean for their businesses. This is compounded by executive timidity about playing a public role in any event. Given the ruthless combat that now mars public life, executives reckon, it's better to keep your head down—especially when change in Washington seems glacially slow, and driven by irrational forces that are hard to control. In addition, too many business leaders have disqualified themselves as public voices through indefensible levels of CEO pay and related scandals. You can't promote the common good if you're seen to care mostly about feathering your own nest.

Then there's a further complication: some business leaders at the helm of global enterprises now feel little direct stake in the quality of public policy in the United States. If 70 percent of your company's sales and profits five years from now will come from overseas, and you can hire the best minds anywhere on the planet to develop your next product, what does it really matter to you if America's schools are failing? It may seem a pity for your country, but it's not a big problem for your business. Finally, most business leaders still operate on the presumption that smaller government, lower taxes, and less regulation are always best for business and the economy. Broadly speaking, they remain firmly in the grip of our Dead Ideas.

But success in business ultimately depends on dealing with the facts, even if they cut against your earlier biases or intuitions. It is precisely this gap between their usual focus on "what works" at the office and their inattention (or knee-jerk reaction) thus far to the broader changes transforming American economic life that gives business leaders enormous potential, once awakened, to help save the day.

The hopeful fact is that business, out of a sense of enlightened self-interest, has embraced this leadership role before. After World

War II, for example, a roster of top executives, via the Committee for Economic Development, helped craft the new policy frameworks, institutions, and political consensus that gave us the postwar boom. Given how gridlocked Washington has become, and the absence of any similarly powerful potential voice today, we won't move from Dead to Destined Ideas fast enough unless business gets off the sidelines, repairs its reputation, reclaims the mantle of statesmanship, and forces both political parties to get serious (or launches a new party that will). Perhaps it's only fitting that the burden of rescuing American capitalism at this crossroads should fall to the capitalists themselves. American executives may not realize it yet, but history is about to summon them to their own rendezvous with destiny.

Breaking the Tyranny of Dead Ideas won't be easy or pretty, but it's coming. The sooner we clear out the cobwebs in our minds, the less jarring and disruptive the years ahead will be, and the less damage these old ways of thinking will inflict on the country. Today we are letting conditions fester that will promote a justified backlash against our economic model and put at risk a system of social organization that has done more to harness human ingenuity for human betterment than any alternative yet imagined. The paradox of our time is that the blind spots of the planet's leading capitalist nation are now the biggest risk to the future of capitalism, and therefore to the well-being not only of the United States but also of billions of people across the globe. We're in a race between capitalism's tendency in this era to wreck so many lives that it loses standing with the public, and our ability to wake up to the stakes, open our minds, and embrace new ways of thinking that make American-style capitalism safe for the twenty-first century.

BURYING DEAD IDEAS
IN BUSINESS AND BEYOND

If all has gone according to plan, you've reached this point convinced that Dead Ideas imperil American civilization and everything we hold dear. But a tiny voice inside may still be asking: What's in it for me? Sure, these old ways of thinking pose threats to your country, your company, and your family. As a citizen you stand ready to move past them and to answer the call of leaders who summon us to see things anew. Yet still you wonder: Isn't there something else I can start doing on Monday? Now that I've got Dead Ideas on the brain, can't I root them out not only in our collective economic and political life, but in my day-to-day life as well?

The answer is yes. The Dead Ideas that surround us operate at different levels. If you work in the business or nonprofit world, the ideas in this book are critical for your enterprise, because they'll define the environment in which your organization will have to operate to be successful. But beyond this external context, unearthing Dead Ideas in your workplace and in your personal life will be increasingly important as well. In an era when more change is expected to occur in the next thirty years than in the previous three hundred, the skill and speed with which people cope with new circumstances will be the key to success; those slow to adapt will be punished faster and more harshly than was the case in calmer times. The logic is plain. If the new pace of change means that the "extinction rate" for the ideas underpinning an organization's success or an individual's well-being are certain to accelerate, it's essential for well-managed firms and well-adjusted people to improve the way they examine their most basic assumptions.

There's no shortage of opportunity here. My own experience suggests that in companies, nonprofits, and government organizations, the Candid Self-Scrutiny muscle is (to put it delicately) underdeveloped. *The indispensable new skill that organizations need to build is a way to institutionalize skeptical thinking, challenges to orthodoxy, and the questioning of fundamental premises.* This is easier said than done, because in many organizations, such behavior can be a career ender. Getting the right organizational mind-set requires a culture and commitment that can only come from the top. Leaders need to embrace this way of thinking and behaving and make it safe for their teams to adopt. The new mantra must be that in an era of accelerating change, *everyone* is at risk of clinging to Dead Ideas that don't reflect new realities. Intellectual inertia is now a permanent occupational hazard.

That's not how most firms act today. Instead, there's often a conspiracy of silence about these basic questions.

A MIND IS A TERRIBLE THING TO CLOSE

Organizations have a hard time revisiting their fundamental assumptions because of what we might call the "three Ps": psychology, politics, and pay. Take psychology first. Behavioral psychologists have identified a decision making phenomenon they call "status quo bias." In one famous test of this effect, people were given a hypothetical inheritance and asked how they would invest it. Some were given a few million dollars in low risk, low return bonds; they generally chose to leave the money alone. Others received a similar amount but in stocks and other riskier securities; and they, too, typically chose to leave the allocation alone. The initial allocation basically governed the outcome, not any taste for risk or approach to investing these people otherwise possessed. The lesson? People basically like to leave things the way they are. Our fear of losing what we have often outweighs our desire to gain from changes we could rationally pursue. In an organizational context, this instinct leads us to spend time and effort cataloguing the risks of trying new things while remaining blind to the risks of staying the current course.

Another feature of organizational psychology that helps Dead Ideas persist is the "false consensus" effect. Researchers point to a number of causes. *Confirmation bias* is the instinct to seek out facts and points of view that support what we already think. *Selective recall* leads us to remember just those experiences and facts that reinforce our assumptions. Thanks to *biased evaluation,* we jump to accept analysis or evidence that supports our view of things, while subjecting contrary evidence to grueling cross-examination, dismissal, or rejection. Then there's *groupthink,* that ineffable pressure to agree with everyone else on a close-knit team. (I don't know about you, but all this sounds like a pretty normal day at the office.)

The second major reason organizations have trouble unearthing their faulty premises is internal politics. When powerful people are in the grip of a flawed idea, it's obviously risky to take them on. My favorite example comes from politics itself. In 1993, President Bill Clinton's economic team felt strongly that the administration's complicated approach to developing a health care plan was bound to fail. Hundreds of people were laboring in a byzantine process that produced a twelve-hundred-page doorstop of a bill. Given that the president's wife was running the process, however, the top economic advisers were not inclined to throw themselves on that particular sword. The result was a fiasco that cost Democrats their majorities in Congress in 1994 and crippled Clinton's presidency.

The third big barrier to rooting out Dead Ideas in organizations is the way people get paid. Corporate compensation schemes often give top executives huge personal incentives to turn a blind eye to the Dead Ideas in their midst, even if it means the company itself is put at risk. The subprime mortgage meltdown was a classic example. At every major bank and investment house, hundreds of top executives made millions in bonuses from profits booked on dodgy mortgage-related securities that were fated to implode. In the words of Charles Prince, the Citigroup CEO who got fabulously rich while presiding over the crippling of this once proud financial giant, "You have to keep dancing until the music stops." Rough translation: ignore the massive risk these mortgage-related securities pose to our institution so long as the money keeps flowing (especially to me). Can anyone doubt that the riches these executives stood to gain clouded their judgment and affected their willingness to acknowledge that the subprime market had become one giant Dead Idea?

The current situation in the pharmaceutical industry (which I have advised) is a subtler but no less compelling example. Big Pharma produces lifesaving medicines we need and want, yet it is viewed less favorably in public opinion polls than the tobacco companies, whose products kill people. This striking state of affairs is the outgrowth of assorted marketing, pricing, research, and lobbying practices that have angered the public and outraged elected officials. It seems clear to many outside observers (including me) that the industry is headed for a regulatory backlash that could undermine the industry's business model and profitability via measures that, however well intended, could also slow the discovery of new drugs. Yet as certain as this coming reckoning seems from outside, the incentives facing individual drug company executives leave them relatively indifferent to it, so long as the bad news hits the fan after their watch. Their compensation arrangements tend to track near-term profitability and share price performance, not the more distant threat of new laws that could fundamentally alter their business, which farsighted changes in their behavior might help them avoid. It's not hard to see the train wreck coming, but no one in the sector has a real incentive to do something about it. From a business point of view it seems bizarre, and unfortunate.

It's an axiom of management that people figure out how to get paid. The upshot? Don't pay people to avoid confronting Dead Ideas that can kill the business.

THE RETURN OF THE COURT JESTER

So: fully aware of these obstacles, what should organizations do if they're serious about rooting out Dead Ideas? As with all important management initiatives, the trick is to get the right people and the right processes in place.

Start with people. Candid self-scrutiny must begin at the top, and that means the board of directors. The diversity of experience represented on well-constructed boards of directors lets them bring perspectives to bear beyond those normally considered by management. The best boards reach into a broad range of a company's constituencies and can tap them for emerging trends and insights that might otherwise go unappreciated, given management's focus on near-term performance.

Once the board has established norms and expectations for confronting and questioning assumptions that may turn out to harbor Dead Ideas, the next critical need is to empower what I think of as *licensed heretics*. These are senior executives or advisers who have a mandate to challenge the organization's sacred cows with impunity, and who have the requisite stature and prestige to assure that their questions and challenges are taken seriously. This role has a long tradition, the most fascinating of which was the court jester in medieval Europe. In addition to providing wit and entertainment, trusted court jesters were known (and valued by the king) for their ability to speak truth to power. "Other court functionaries cooked up the king's facts for him before delivery," said one royal insider hundreds of years ago. "The jester delivered them raw." I'm not saying every licensed heretic has to be a song and dance man, though tact and a sense of humor surely help. But I am trying to suggest the creative space needed in an organization to make this role flourish. (In our public life, this role is notably filled today by Jon Stewart and *The Daily Show,* whose political analysis is routinely more insightful and subversive than anything offered by the regular news media.)

The way this role is implemented will obviously vary by organization. Some CEOs may believe some of their direct reports can fulfill it, though career considerations usually limit the degree of candor that's possible in these relationships. Another approach is to establish senior roles without line responsibility in the office of the CEO. This nonoperating "counselor" role is quite common in the White House; David Gergen, for example, served Bill Clinton in this role during a critical period in his first term after the president had lost his footing, and Gergen's independence, experience, and judgment proved a critical (if also internally controversial) help. But such "wise men" can also fail: Robert Rubin of Citigroup, for example, was widely criticized when as a (lavishly paid) corporate consigliere he did nothing to avert the firm's disastrous plunge into the mortgage mess.

Outsiders can also be invited to act as the licensed heretic. In a number of large school districts, for example, superintendents use an adviser that school reformers call a "critical friend." This is not a full-time role, but a trusted counselor (often a successful retired superintendent) who in regular sessions brings to bear facts and perspectives meant to assist the current school leader in keeping his plans on track. Superintendents tell me that when the role works well, it's because the critical friend's only agenda is to improve the district's performance; his value stems from his stature, discretion, and willingness to force the school leader to face unpleasant truths.

From my own experience as a consultant, it's clear that outsiders have advantages in playing this role. Once, for example, I was asked to talk to the CEO of a large financial services firm about some challenges the company was facing. The situation essentially required me to clash with this strong-willed leader for ninety minutes in order to persuade him that he wasn't thinking about things in the right way. As an outsider who cared about the institution I was free to take him on with the kind of intensity and persistence that his own people couldn't have risked, and it helped him see things differently. After this session, other executives came up to me to say, "It's so great you told him *x* or *y*—he'd never hear that the same way inside." Even outside heretics can have their heads handed to them now and then, but the impact one can have is considerable.

However the role is structured, those asked to perform it must remember above all that there are *no dumb questions*. The Dead Ideas in this book become apparent, for example, only when we ask dumb questions like "Why do we assume taxes always hurt the economy?" or "Why should employers be in the business of offering health benefits anyway?" Peter Drucker, the legendary management guru, always asked seemingly innocent questions. What business are you in? Who are your customers? Who do you want them to be? As he helped teach us, the "dumbest" questions are almost always the smartest questions, because they get at the fundamentals.

The bottom line is that there are many ways to skin the cat here. What's important is to recognize the need to have this licensed heretic function, and to find a viable way of stitching it into the organization. Top executives also need to know that in this era of rapid change they *need* someone to play this role, for their own good and for their firm's.

DEAD IDEAS WANTED!

Just having the right people in this role isn't enough, however. There also need to be mechanisms in place, either as part of the board's calendar of activities or as a supplement to the company's strategic planning process, that assures regular attention to these questions. One approach would be to put in place what I call a Dead Idea Assessment. The idea would be to engage an organization's senior team, and also its most promising younger executives, in an exercise that challenges core premises and slays sacred cows. The Dead Idea Assessment would step back to get crystal clear on the critical assumptions underlying the business. Why do we think they're still valid, or will be in a couple of years? What forces may render them obsolete? What opportunities are we missing because of our current (but dated) convictions? What might we do differently if we knew their days were numbered?

A Dead Idea Assessment might have three phases. In phase one, executives across the organization would be asked to nominate candidates for the "Dead Idea Watch List." A team leading the assessment would narrow the list down to those that seem central to the organization's future and merit further scrutiny. In phase two, teams would be assigned to assess whether an idea was in fact dead, by tracing the idea's history in the industry or firm and analyzing how new and foreseeable circumstances affect its relevance and validity. (This is the process of understanding "the story" of the idea, as we did earlier in this book for our Dead Ideas on the economy.) The teams would also be asked to reach for new ways of thinking by suggesting successors to ideas they conclude are dinosaurs. In the third phase, the various ideas' "proximity to death" might be ranked—some ideas might be judged already dead, some put on a "watch list," and some seen to be surprisingly alive and kicking upon closer inspection. The insights generated by these dialogues and analyses would help shape the firm's priorities going forward.

An example can help make the potential power of such a process concrete. In the early 1990s, United Parcel Service, the longtime industry leader in ground package shipping, was looking to build its nascent air express business. Federal Express was the market leader. UPS at that time did not offer discounts to large-volume air shippers: a catalog company that shipped five hundred packages a day, for example, paid the same price per package as a grandmother who shipped one overnight letter to her grandchild each year. A Dead Idea that might have surfaced in a regular assessment would have been, "Offering the same price to all customers regardless of volume is fair, and doesn't hurt our revenue and profit potential." The "story" would document how this was the way things had always been done at UPS; the uniform price actually reflected a deep cultural commitment to treating customers "fairly." A potential successor idea might have been, "Only lower prices can lead to higher profits." This would form the hypothesis to be tested and refined with further analysis. What UPS found (which it knew at some level, but had not focused on) is that it costs much less to serve high volume shippers, and that offering them sharply lower prices to reflect this reality was a different yet entirely defensible way of thinking about "fairness" to particular customers. Market research confirmed that such discounting would bring huge new revenues and profits. In the end, this is the course UPS eventually pursued, and its air business grew enormously. Scrutinizing the business through this lens of Dead Ideas is a powerful way to ferret out ingrained assumptions that people never stop to question. The way the "storytelling" aspect of such an assessment can shine a light on intangibles (such as UPS's value of fairness) suggests the richness it can bring in ways that help build consensus for new directions.

DEAD IDEAS CLOSER TO HOME

Outside big companies, scrutiny of Dead Ideas can generate new business opportunities as well. For years my wife, Jody, decried the idea held by most big companies that "you have to own 100 percent of talented businesspeople in order to make effective use of them." Jack Welch of General Electric represented the apotheosis of this old-school thinking, under which the job of a great leader was to allocate capital and grow this wholly owned internal talent over time. In Jody's view, this model of talent deployment was dying; in the future, she was convinced, the best managers and firms would be the ones that pulled diverse expertise together when they needed it and then disbanded it when they didn't. Corporations would become more fluid and permeable to meet business's evolving need for flexibility and nimbleness, as well as talented people's desire for more control over their lives outside the traditional "all or nothing" corporate career track. There was only one problem: no infrastructure existed to allow this to happen. Jody thus launched the Business Talent Group in 2007 to create a marketplace that didn't exist—a way to quickly match (in five days) the best independent business professionals with companies that have consulting, interim executive, or project-based needs. Today her growing firm serves clients nationally from offices in Los Angeles, New York, San Francisco, and Seattle. What her clients are saying, in effect, is that Jody's business is a Destined Idea. And it was born, naturally enough, out of frustration with a Dead Idea.

My wife provides a nice segue to a brief final word on dealing with Dead Ideas in your personal life. Every married person knows these exist, and can fester. Every parent knows their children think they (the parents) are hopelessly blinded by Dead Ideas, which helps explain why parents are so embarrassing to have around. The biggest Dead Idea I've learned that I am in the grip of at home is that My Daughter (who is eleven as I write this) Is Still a Little Girl. I know this not thanks to any formal Dead Idea Assessment, mind you. In our house, the way it works is that my wife and daughter scream "She's not a little girl anymore!" until I get it.

I'm exaggerating a little, but not about the role Dead Ideas ultimately play in all our lives. Ever since Freud, the path to personal growth and self-improvement has involved efforts to unearth aspects of our unconscious mind that hold us back. Progress means facing up to thoughts and feelings we've repressed so deeply that we're no longer aware of them. Perhaps you see the circle I am trying to close. If individuals can be stuck in certain modes of behavior because of emotional patterns they developed when they were young, little wonder that the American economy finds itself stuck in certain patterns because of ideas we got hooked on long ago. In the end, resolving to overcome Dead Ideas offers hope because it means facing up to an essential vulnerability in our nature. If I'm right, the eventful decade ahead will play out like any other exercise in therapy, but with 300 million minds on the couch. For people, organizations, or nations, the perils of being trapped in old thinking are the same. And the first step toward a cure is admitting that we need help.

ACKNOWLEDGMENTS

Thanks are due first to the Center for American Progress, which has been my public policy home since 2003, and which provided financial and research support for this book. John Podesta, CAP's president, offered encouragement and ideas from the beginning, as did Sarah Rosen Wartell, Melody Barnes, Nina Hachigian, Cassandra Butts, and Anna Soellner. Amanda Logan, Christian Weller, and Luke Reidenbach helped with research. Cindy Brown encouraged me to adapt early work on the education chapter into a CAP report, which became the basis for a panel discussion in Washington that helped further refine my thinking.

Lucy Moore provided additional research assistance. Linda Laucella ably transcribed dozens of interviews. Carl Kaestle and Benjamin Friedman took time from their busy schedules to read drafts of chapters and offer thoughtful critiques.

I was fortunate to be able to try out early versions of some of the thinking in *The Tyranny of Dead Ideas* in several magazines. Thanks in this regard to James Bennet and Amy Meeker at *The*

Atlantic Monthly and to Rick Stengel at *Time.* At *Fortune,* thanks to Andy Serwer, Jim Aley, and Steve Koepp, as well as to two previous managing editors of *Fortune,* Eric Pooley and Rik Kirkland. A number of ideas were also honed via weekly jousting on the public radio program "Left, Right & Center." Thanks to my longtime radio cronies Bob Scheer, Arianna Huffington, and Tony Blankley, as well as to our intrepid producer, Sarah Spitz, and to Ruth Seymour, the general manager at our remarkable home station, KCRW-FM, in Santa Monica.

Dozens of people and books who helped shape my thinking are discussed or quoted in the text. Others to whom I'm grateful for helpful conversations include: Michael Barber, Doug Beck, Eric Beinhocker, Bill Bradley, Alan Brinkley, David Card, Larry Cohen, Jon Cowan, David Cutler, Leslie Dach, Sharon Davies, Robert Driskill, Tom Epstein, Richard Freeman, William Gale, Pete Galier, Alan Garber, Julius Genachowski, Gina Glantz, Austan Goolsbee, Robert Gordon, Kati Haycock, Doug Irwin, Jennifer Klein, Bob Kocher, Andrew Kohut, Charles Kolb, Robert Lawrence, Edward Lazarus, Robert Litan, Alan Michaels, Ted Mitchell, Joel Mokyr, Len Nichols, Louise Novotny, Peter Orzsag, James Patterson, Diane Ravitch, Frank Sammartino, Isabel Sawhill, Andrew Stern, Peter Swenson, Peter Temin, David Tyack, Steve Weisman, Sean Wilentz, Ron Wyden, Andrew Yarrow, and Julian Zelizer. I'm also especially grateful for the support and intellectual camaraderie offered by Lenny Mendonca, Michael Stewart, Larry Kanarek, Byron Auguste, Nick Lovegrove, and Michael Patsalos-Fox.

The Times Books division of Henry Holt and Company is a terrific place to publish. I feel lucky to have worked with my editor, Paul Golob. This is our second collaboration, and his close reading and wise counsel (again) improved the book. Dan Farley, Holt's president and publisher, was an enthusiast throughout, as was his predecessor, John Sterling. Thanks also to the rest of the Holt team, including Maggie Richards, Claire McKinney, Emily Belford,

Tara Kennedy, Denise Cronin, Eileen Lawrence, Richard Rhorer, and Pearl Wu. Copy editor Emily DeHuff provided many helpful suggestions.

Thanks to my literary agent, Philippa Brophy, for making the business side of the book a breeze (and for giving it to me straight when an earlier version of the proposal that eventually became *The Tyranny of Dead Ideas* was itself lacking a pulse).

Quite by accident this book was written while we were doing a major home renovation, something I would not advise people to do, especially if (like me) you work at home. Still, our contractors, Marc Futterman and Bill Shaw, and our architects, Nathalie Aragno and William Hefner, deserve thanks for putting up with my surly moods, threatening e-mails, screaming bouts, and periods of inexplicable withdrawal, only some of which were entirely justified.

My mother, Marianne Miller, and my father and stepmother, Tim and Simone Miller, offered constant love and support. My in-laws, Lynn and Emil Hubschman and Albert and Judy Greenstone, were endlessly encouraging. My sister-in-law, Tracy Drufovka, provided keen insider perspectives on health care. Our daughter's nanny, Zoila Benitez, once again helped keep our family sane during a hectic time.

My wife and daughter make everything possible and worthwhile. Amelia, now eleven and fantabulous in every way, had the original idea for a broken light bulb as the cover art, and introduced me to the "Miniature Earth" Web site and presentation cited in chapter 7. (In my own research I came across something useful for her school report on Chester Alan Arthur, so this isn't just a one-way thing.) Amelia took so seriously my admonition that good writing means simple words that she rightly upbraided me for all the big boring ones she saw on the screen whenever she checked on Daddy's progress. Amelia also bucked me up with the mantra she has usefully imbibed about this kind of work at an early age. "Writing isn't writing," she would lecture impishly. "*Re*-writing is writing." Amelia also designed a clever Mad Lib on the book as a holiday gift, leaving this volume forever known around our house as "The Tyranny of Fiendish Shoes."

My wife, Jody, the love of my life, is the indispensable woman, supplying endless quantities of love, insight, and stroking of the authorial ego. But there's more. It can be a little demoralizing to be married to someone who you often think could do your job better than you do, even while she simultaneously renovates a house, mothers your child, and leads a start-up business. Sometimes I think Jody must be one of those superior life forms like they had in the original *Star Trek* series, who assume human shape only in order to be able to communicate with the oafish earthlings. Besides all the romantic and parental good stuff, Jody is the sharpest thinker and editor a writer could dream of having close at hand, which probably explains a lot. If the analysis and arguments in this book have some merit, it's largely because Jody hammered them (and me) into better shape. Thanks for everything, sweetheart.

INDEX

ABOUT THE AUTHOR

MATT MILLER is a contributing editor to *Fortune*, a senior fellow at the Center for American Progress, and the host of public radio's popular week-in-review program, *Left, Right & Center*. A former White House aide during the Clinton administration, he is a consultant to corporations, governments, and nonprofits. His first book, *The Two Percent Solution: Fixing America's Problems in Ways Liberals and Conservatives Can Love,* was a *Los Angeles Times* bestseller. He lives in Los Angeles with his wife, Jody Greenstone Miller, the founder and CEO of the Business Talent Group, and their daughter.